Essentials of Literacy from 0–7

Education at SAGE

SAGE is a leading international publisher of journals, books, and electronic media for academic, educational, and professional markets.

Our education publishing includes:

- accessible and comprehensive texts for aspiring education professionals and practitioners looking to further their careers through continuing professional development

- inspirational advice and guidance for the classroom

- authoritative state of the art reference from the leading authors in the field

Find out more at: **www.sagepub.co.uk/education**

2nd Edition

Essentials of Literacy from 0–7

A WHOLE-CHILD APPROACH TO COMMUNICATION, LANGUAGE AND LITERACY

TINA BRUCE and JENNY SPRATT

Los Angeles | London | New Delhi
Singapore | Washington DC

First edition published 2008
Reprinted 2009
This second edition first published 2011

SAGE Publications Ltd
1 Oliver's Yard
55 City Road
London EC1Y 1SP

SAGE Publications Inc.
2455 Teller Road
Thousand Oaks, California 91320

SAGE Publications India Pvt Ltd
B 1/I 1 Mohan Cooperative Industrial Area
Mathura Road
New Delhi 110 044

SAGE Publications Asia-Pacific Pte Ltd
3 Church Street
#10-04 Samsung Hub
Singapore 049483

Library of Congress Control Number: 2010934966

British Library Cataloguing in Publication data

A catalogue record for this book is available from the British Library

ISBN 978-1-84920-598-6
ISBN 978-1-84920-599-3 (pbk)

Typeset by C&M Digitals (P) Ltd, Chennai, India
Printed and bound in Great Britain by Ashford Color Press Ltd
Printed on paper from sustainable resources

Contents

About the Authors

Tina Bruce CBE is an honorary visiting professor at Roehampton University, having originally trained as a teacher at the Froebel Educational Institute. She was head of the Froebel Research Nursery School in the Froebel College, becoming Director of the Centre for Early Childhood Studies. She has worked with the British Council in New Zealand and Egypt, and was awarded *International Woman Scholar* by the University of Virginia Commonwealth. She is involved with training and consultancy for the Early Childhood Phase in the UK, China and Soweto in South Africa. She is a Vice-president of the British Association for Early Childhood, and a Trustee of the Froebel Council and the National Froebel Foundation.

Jenny Spratt is Head of Birth to 7 Services in an English Local Authority where she has led the Early Years and Childcare Strategy since 1998. She has a background in Early Childhood Education and was Headteacher of a Nursery School for nine years. She represents the Local Authority Early Years Network on the Early Childhood Forum, which is co-ordinated through the National Children's Bureau and was a member of the Centre for Excellence and Outcomes (C4EO) Early Years Theme Advisory Group. She is also a Trustee of the National Froebel Foundation and acts as an Early Years and Child Poverty sector specialist for C4EO.

Introduction and Acknowledgements

Every few years, there seems to be a passionate debate about literacy in England. Why? There are all sorts of reason for this.

- Governments fear that unless workers are literate, England will not be able to compete in the world with other countries (Brown, 2007; Gove, 2010).
- Experts in literacy, or aspects of literacy, often believe children are badly taught because different methods are favoured from the ones they advocate. They seek to influence official approaches to literacy, with the result that across the years there has been great variety as different approaches gain the upper hand (Bullock, 1975; DfEE, 1998, 2007; Rose, 2006).
- Parents, grandparents and the public in general become very confused by all of the various 'expert' views on how children should be taught to read and write.
- Practitioners rarely engage in all the battles about literacy (Hall, 2007), but they do find it difficult to ascertain, among all the experts, who to trust and who is 'right'. They simply wish to do their best for the children and families they work with.

Who knows what about literacy – and who is 'right'?

When interconnected knowledge and understanding work in close harmony with tried and tested practice wisdom, then practitioners and parents will work well together. The result is that children will then flourish in their development and learning.

To bring this about, practitioners need regularly to review and reflect on practice, and to see whether it is in tune with new developments in the understanding of both child development and subject knowledge. Inevitably, we find that we need to make some adjustments and changes.

But the changes need to be interconnected to make a consistent, logically coherent whole. If we are totally disconnected from what we have known previously we shall end up in a muddle, unable to see clearly the best ways to link with what is new.

Becoming a community of learners, adults and children together

The first edition of this book came about because of a resurgence of interest in the teaching of reading owing to the (2007) Rose review on reading. Eighteen local authorities accepted the invitation to participate in the Department for Education and Skills' (DfES) National Pilot of Early Reading Development (DfES, 2005b), which was based on exploring a systematic approach to the teaching of phonics. Since then the work has developed and in this second edition of the book (written because of the demand that ensued following the success of the first edition) we have been able to consolidate and take forward the work that was begun in 2005. Over five years, using the approach outlined in this book – as well as and together with time-honoured early childhood practices – consistently across the local authority, the 'Communication, Language and Literacy' scores on the *Early Years Foundation Stage Profile* have improved by 14% (compared with a national improvement of 8%). It has been exciting and heartening to see such progress in our understanding of a child's journey of communication and language development and then reading and writing.

Working together – the first year

For a full year, the authors and teachers in the pedagogy team in one of the 18 local authorities worked with practitioners in the private, voluntary, and independent (PVI) sectors. The settings were chosen because they linked up with primary schools that the local authority had selected to take part in the DfES project.

The head of Early Years and Childcare then decided this work should develop over two years (rather than the one year of the DfES pilot). Since then she has, with her team, organized a third year of training in order to share the work we did together with the whole PVI sector and with receiving schools invited to join in. This has now become part of the way the team works, and Reception class teachers have reported that they feel more linked and connected.

Working together – the second year

During the second year of our work together (2006) the *Early Years Foundation Stage (EYFS)* was finalized (DfES, 2007a), becoming the legally-enshrined official curriculum framework for children from birth to five years of age in England in September 2008. It was this document which was to guide those who were taking part in the renamed Communication, Language and Literacy Development Project.

The early years literacy specialist from the Learning and Standards Team in the local authority was formally invited to join the project and, by the summer, Reception teachers and Year 1 teachers were linking and attending meetings, and asking to be included in the third year of the training.

Working together – the third year

Practitioners who have participated in the first two years are helping us to mainstream the training by talking about their work and also by encouraging visits from the new participants so that everyone can learn from each other. Teachers in Reception and Year 1 classes, encouraged by those who attended the training at the end of the second year, have requested to join us. The leading teachers, with their team leader from Learning and Standards have, to our delight, asked to participate once again. A Reception teacher has also contributed case studies for the second edition of the book.

This book is about our continuing work together. We are interweaving the requirements of the official, legally enshrined documents with traditional early childhood approaches, and adjusting our practice as we respond to recent research on communication, language and literacy.

Into the future, taking along treasure from the past and adding new knowledge

We locate Communication, Language and Literacy in a multi-sensory, rich communication and language environment and nest phonics within this as one aspect of it. We had to do some thinking, and to adjust in order to update our practice without throwing away any treasure from the past that needed to be kept. The principles still held but we could see that the practice needed to develop.

The four countries of the UK have developed their early childhood framework documents in different ways. The English framework began its review, chaired by Dame Clare Tickell, in August 2010. In Scotland, Wales and Northern Ireland there is emphasis on the heritage of the country and its language. In England this is less in evidence. This framework, after review, will then be reframed and we shall continue our work into the future. It is an important principle that official documents and policies should never dictate how practitioners work. They are a resource to be used and integrated into what is previously known. In this way of working the arrival of a constant flow of new official documents is not overwhelming. It allows for continuity in what is found to remain important after reviewing and reflecting. It also means that this kind of reflection assists the possibility of changing practice so that it is in tune with current theory and practice and in order that it is is interwoven with the philosophy that binds the work together in a consistent whole.

Introducing the community of learners

- The authors – Jenny Spratt, Head of Early Years and Childcare in the local authority and Tina Bruce, the external Early Childhood Consultant.
- Contributions were made by the Early Years and Childcare Team members led by Susan Cary and Karen Hingston. These were Jacki Yetzes, Emma Brader, Lesley Evans (part-time), Julia Robinson, Andrea Gamman, Alii Collier, and Kim Neilson, leading the training on 'Communicating Matters' (DfES). Also Heather Fry, speech and language therapist with the Early Years Inclusion Team, Alison Wallace, Alison Riley, Emma Woollard, Steve Wells, Sallyann Hilliard, Annie Hornsby, Jo Smith, Syreeta Payne, Catrina Storey, Cathy Ruffles, Gill Davies, Zelda Eldred and Marilyn Rogers.
- Janet Lavender and Tricia Shingles (music input) were also contributors from the sector.
- Research partners (as the teachers working with the settings were called) were: Margaret Emerson and Cathy Ruffles, Sally Atkinson, Helen Norris, Gill Roberts, Susan Cary and Alison Carroll.
- Seven voluntary managed playgroups participated.
- Case studies were provided by Reception teacher, Sarah Taylor.

Glinton Pre-School Playgroup, Supervisor Jane Ringham and Leigh-Anne Goodliffe, pre-school assistant

Helping a child overcome a fear of spiders through a project built around the rhyme 'Incy Wincy Spider' gives the language of feelings

New Ark Playgroup, Supervisor Elizabeth Buck and Linda Wilson, Deputy Supervisor

The emphasis on the outdoor area in this setting (where staff are trained in the forest school approach) led to children being encouraged to have phone conversations out of doors. This especially attracts boys, who enjoy chatting in this way

Orton Wistow Under Fives Playgroup, Manager Donna Pickavance

Sharing learning and sustained conversations between parents, practitioners and children who know each other well

Noah's Ark Pre-School, Manager Jacqueline Weaver

Home-made props engage both children and staff. Here these are used out of doors

South Bretton Pre-School – Middleton, Manager Judy Flynn

Using small world 'menu' cards, so that children can use these with props in their spontaneous play

Parnwell Pre-School, Jan Jukes

Real experiences that support the words of the rhymes and poetry cards and also make sense and meaning for children, who may well not know what pease pudding is and who may never have seen a pig or a market. Adapting words and giving meaningful experiences are important essentials of literacy

Rainbow Pre-School, Manager Janice Foulkes Arnold

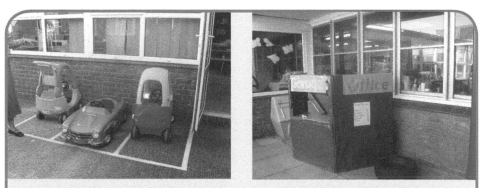

Story boxes and props for free-flow play scenarios are an invaluable resource for practitioners to build up. They encourage children to revisit rhymes and poetry cards, and to vary the themes and create their own. The props help children not to lose the plot or the words of the rhyme as part of a multi-sensory and rich enabling environment

One childminder (in the Childminders' Network), Julie Brown

Broad rich learning is emphasized. Children will often choose to paint or make models of characters such as Humpty Dumpty

Mark-making – a beginning for letters in his name

Caverstede, a maintained nursery school in the LA (which is also a children's centre). Lucy King and Nicole Gough, a teacher and nursery nurse team. See photos above

- During the second year we were joined by Mary Purdon (Learning and Standards), who, with her team of leading teachers, Carly Tilney, Linda Harries and Kathryn Gray, worked closely with us, the Reception classes and Year 1.
- At the end of the second year, the majority of the teachers in Reception and Year 1 joined us (Samantha Keene from Parnwell Primary School, Jo Simpson from Newark Hill Primary School, Tracey Petherick from Queen's Drive Infant School, Karyn Hillier from Peakirk-cum-Ginton Primary School), Carly Tilney and Linda Harries from Orton Wistow Primary School. They asked to be included in the future training we have developed for the third year.

The importance of a rich language environment, with multi-sensory experiences

Boys engaging with early communication, language and literacy

It was interesting that the local authority had an unusually high number of summer-born boys, and we were concerned that they should not be put under inappropriate pressure to read and write. We therefore emphasized the importance of:

- movement experiences (Greenland, 2006)
- three-dimensional props
- real experiences relating to the props for rhymes.

We found that boys were becoming more interested and involved in aspects of the development and learning that related to literacy and literature.

We hope that from now on – with more practitioners joining the training and greater links with the Reception and Year 1 teachers – we shall take this work forward with a positive effect. By this however we do not mean we want children to start reading and writing earlier and earlier. We mean that we have been delighted by the way boys and girls are engaging with and enjoying communicating and developing language, in addition to developing the essentials of reading and writing – hopefully as lifelong pursuits.

A broad, rich and deep curriculum, across all areas of development and learning

We are helping children to develop as communicating people, socially and emotionally, creatively, linguistically, physically and in their movement co-ordination, mathematics, reasoning and problem-solving, as well as their knowledge and understanding of the world. Our work goes beyond narrow literacy training.

The experiences we are giving the children are there to support learning in all these aspects. Good early childhood practice is not narrow practice. It deepens and expands learning in many ways.

> The most reassuring aspect of the Communication, Language and Literacy programme is that children have made the most progress in their phonic development in schools where there is excellent early provision: where phonics is not taught in isolation but embedded in opportunities to read and write that are meaningful for the children and developed by them.
>
> We are providing them with the tools to communicate, a way of coding what they want to say, but not restricting how or what they do. The writing that children produce is in their own words, not following an adult structure, but reflecting the rich language of their play. These children know that they can communicate, and are confident learners. They are ready to fly! (Mary Purdon from the Learning and Standards Team in the local authority)

By the end of the Foundation Stage, she reported that most children in Reception classes were enjoying sharing books and choosing to look at these with spontaneous interest. They possessed a good understanding of the alphabetic code, linking sounds and graphemes, and were engaged. They came to Key Stage 1 with a real enjoyment of sounds and words, and enthusiastically explored and experimented with these. They were more aware of similarities and differences in sound and the sources of these than previous groups had been. They also had a love of alliteration, rhythm and rhyme.

One of the most important things has been the way in which different teams have linked and dialogued together:

> For the past two years, I have been working in Reception classes on the National 'Communication, Language and Literacy Development' programme. I have changed my thinking about children's progress and my expectations of children's achievement in the area of communication, language and literacy. These children from the pre-schools are entering Reception with a greater desire to link sounds and letters, engage with rhyming and rhythmic experiences and participate in meaningful mark making. After the initial year, schools were reporting significant gains in many areas, but particularly in linking sounds and letters. With the work being further embedded in the second year these gains seem to have increased. (Leading teacher, Kathryn Gray)

Susan Cary, Manager, Early Childhood Pedagogy

> Much of our focus and thinking has been on ensuring a smooth transition for children in Reception moving into Year 1 in Key Stage 1. With better observation based record-keeping in the *EYFS* by Reception Class teachers, which now identifies the phases that children are currently working within in their reading and writing, there can be a smoother transition into Key Stage 1.

Their conversation together echoes Marie Clay:

> At entry to school, children have been learning for five years, since they were born. They are ready to learn more than they already know. Why do schools and educators find this so difficult to understand? Teachers must find out what children already know, and take them from where they are to somewhere else. (1993: 5)

This means that an understanding within both sectors (schools and PVI settings) of the children and the subject knowledge is required if a true picture of each child is to be built which will inform a teacher's planning in Year 1.

An exchange of information between the settings, schools, parents and carers is essential through the sharing of examples of work and discussion on individual children's progress.

Karen Hingston, Manager, Early Years Childcare Team

> The Communication, Language and Literacy Project has had a huge impact on the way my team and I view our work with early years settings. It has really broadened our view, appreciating it involves everyone and everything that is done within the setting, being integral to all that is

provided, the environment, the practitioners and the support they are given. Working together across teams has also had a tremendous impact on developing all our understanding and proved invaluable. We all need to think about what and how we provide for children from the earliest age and the impact this has.

Learning together, adults and children

We are a learning community, in the sense that Michael Barber describes (see Stannard and Huxford, 2007: 6). Our training together has led us to the importance of practitioners understanding:

- the biologically driven aspects of child development
- the social and cultural aspects of developing learning
- the subject knowledge practitioners need to enable them to develop the essentials of literacy with other people's children and parents/carers
- the importance of rich learning environments, involving relationships, ideas and feelings as well as the physical sense of self.

In the nineteenth century the educational pioneer Friedrich Froebel created learning communities in his schools in which he advised practitioners and parents, 'Let us live with our children, learning from them as well as teaching them'.

THOUGHTS TO TAKE WITH YOU AS YOU READ THE BOOK

It is likely that experienced practitioners reading the book will find it, in the main, reaffirming. There may be new things to reflect on and consider, too, as there have been for us. We have adjusted our practice, but that is part of being in a learning community.

For all practitioners, we hope that we have helpfully captured the excitement of children's journeys into literacy, literature and new knowledge and understanding. The essentials of literacy are about educating children in the deepest sense. We owe it to children to know as much as we can:

- about how children develop and learn
- about how their family and culture and community value literacy
- about acquiring and updating our subject knowledge of what is involved in becoming literate
- about valuing professional development as a key part of this.

Working with other people's children – and their parents – requires us to be as highly trained, educated, measured and mature as possible. All of these are parts of the essentials of literacy.

Summary – the essentials of literacy

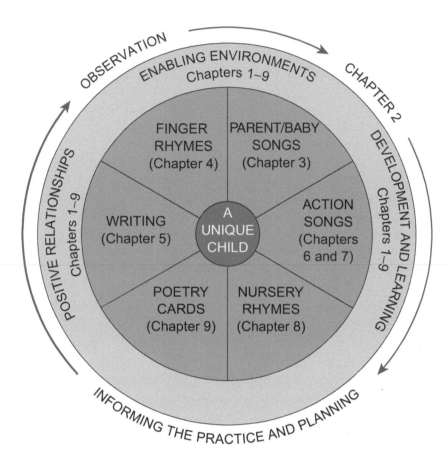

This chart summarizes the book. It shows those areas of communication, language and literacy that we worked on together as a group

Chapter **1**

Introducing the Essentials of Communication, Language and Literacy

In this chapter we show how:

- reading and writing rest on the foundations of communication and language development;
- not every child will develop language or learn to read and write, but with support most children with special needs can learn to communicate;
- there are many diverse activities through which we help children into literacy;
- literacy teaching thrives in an encouraging and relaxed environment linked to the whole curriculum.

When should children be taught to read and write?

In most cultures of the world, literacy (being able to read and write, either in print or Braille or by using computer technological aids) is important and considered necessary for a full participation in society, and in order for each person living in that society to make a contribution. It is seen as a key to knowledge and understanding ideas, or reflection on feelings and relationships through information and literature.

Opening up the world of knowledge and understanding and finding there is lifelong satisfaction in communicating, with and without words, and in reading and writing, also equips children for survival in a fast-developing global world economy where the future is uncertain and unknown.

It involves:

- good communication (sensitive use of words/signs, body language, saying things without words)
- rich language (being articulate and being a sensitive listener)
- becoming a bookworm who reads avidly both for pleasure and for information
- writing mainly for pleasure (greetings to family and friends) and for other reasons as well
- writing so as to share ideas, put forward arguments, campaign, and reaffirm ideas.

In most countries of the world, children are between 6 and 7 years old when they are taught to read and write, because that is a good time biologically, and typically they then learn to do so within about three months. By this age language (either spoken or signed), unless there are socio-cultural challenges or disabilities, will be established. Articulation has developed, so that children can hear and say the sounds of a language. As speech and language specialists remind us, pronunciation and phonological awareness is linked to how children will tackle the links between phonics and graphics that are so central to being able to read and write. Having a wide enough vocabulary, and being able to say what you mean (the semantics) is crucial too. Children can be taught to bark at print, but reading with and for meaning is what it is all about. Language is hardwired to develop in the brain. The processes of reading and writing are not (Carter, 1999). Reading and writing depend on language in order to get going (as it were), and they piggyback onto language as they develop.

Do children (provided they are given a rich learning environment) learn to read and write naturally?

One view is that children will learn to read and write quite naturally, but only if they are in an environment that encourages this through:

- people around them reading and writing
- being read to
- engaging with literature and informational print as an important part of everyday life.

Parents might read a newspaper regularly, or at weekends. As they grow up children will see this focussed attention, and perhaps hear the various comments their mother or father makes about news items. They might see their parents making shopping lists and choosing programmes to watch on television or to listen to on the radio. They might also see them paying bills, writing in cheque books, or more often nowadays, writing on line at the computer. All this establishes an important backcloth that will in turn encourage children to engage with books and the mark-making which leads into writing.

Bedtime stories (Brice-Heath, 1983) can give children the opportunity to ask questions, and comment as they go, within an atmosphere of warm affection. Not all children are read to in this way, but there can be other times of day when stories can be read to them. Indeed such bedtime stories might be more practical for working parents. Kathy Goouch (in Goouch and Lambirth, 2007) writes about the way a group of graduate parents introduced their children to reading, writing, literature and information-seeking in exactly this way. Their children then possessed a rich language as a base on which to build their literacy development.

Involving children in writing shopping lists – perhaps making their parallel list in their own way, with their own marks and drawings – means that children are participating and becoming part of a writing community, in a relaxed and unpressured way. This is done in the spirit of everyone being involved, and the child is not expected to perform but to join in, doing what they can without being judged for how successfully they achieve adult ways of writing or reading. Having a go is the important thing, with the child's efforts being taken seriously.

Friedrich Froebel (1782–1852) pioneered the thinking that children can learn a huge amount about communication, language and literacy when they share songs and finger rhymes with their parents. He called these the 'Mother Songs'. Had he been alive today he would doubtless have included fathers too, but at that point in history the emphasis was on the role of mothers in the informal and natural education of children. The idea was to build on nature, with children's natural enjoyment of rhymes, songs and stories as part of family life.

Johannella Tafuri (2008: 1) researched the musical development of young children who had been sung to in the womb. She, like Froebel, emphasized the importance of family singing, as it has 'anthropological, cultural and social value in all cultures'.

Should children be taught to read as early as possible?

Another point of view is that children need to be inducted into reading and writing and the earlier the better. The argument is that becoming independent readers and writers as young as possible gives them the key to the door which opens up the world of literature and knowledge to them. They are then not dependent on others reading to them, or writing on their behalf. Until they can read fluently they are thought to find chunks of text confusing and therefore be unable to appreciate literature or non-fiction texts fully. The emphasis is on being able to read and write without help, rather than on Vygotsky's (1978) notion of practitioners needing to aim their teaching, as he puts it, at the 'ripening buds' rather than the 'opened flowers' in order that children do not have to perform early but are supported by adults in their understanding. Sometimes their competence will develop steadily, sometimes in a burst, and sometimes it will plateau as if pausing for breath. Learning does not develop at the same pace throughout.

Key moments in the journey towards literacy

Is it important for practitioners to know about the biological, social and cultural development of children, and the subject knowledge of what is involved in literacy, literature and the seeking and sharing of knowledge and information, so they can learn how to put the two together in order to help children read and write.

The view of this book is that biologically-driven processes are a vital part of learning how to read and write. Without a body and a brain there is no question of this being possible! But we cannot just leave things to nature. Neuroscientist Colin Blakemore (2001) argues that **'nurture shapes nature'**. This means that there are important processes functioning both in the brain, and in the growing and maturing body. If we work with these we can help children to develop their learning with maximum impact. Our biological selves are shaped and nurtured by people, relationships and culture. This is particularly the case where reading and writing are concerned. We are not leaving things to nature – instead, we are working with nature.

We need to understand what is involved in the subject knowledge of literacy. What are the essentials of texts and how do they work? What are the mechanics of reading and writing? Some of the most important things in developing literacy are not always that obvious. The way the brain works to co-ordinate vision, hearing and movement is crucial here and so is the way each child develops as a symbol maker and symbol user. Talking, understanding what others say, and engaging in conversations are each part of this process.

The co-ordination of the hands, looking and hearing

How hands, ears and eyes will begin to co-ordinate is an important part of the journey into language and from there into literacy, literature, knowledge and information. (This will be explored in Chapter 3.)

Walking, talking and pretending: the excitement and celebration of the first steps in walking

When a baby becomes a toddler, and takes his or her first steps, family and friends will become awash with excitement – and so they should. This co-ordination of the body's movements is one of the greatest landmarks towards literacy. By the time a toddler reaches this point in life, the long journey into communication, language and literacy will be well under way.

In her study of children singing in their families, and where a mother sang while her baby was in the womb, Johannella Tafuri (2008: 83) found that 71% of the 3-year-olds could sing in tune. This was of interest because children at this age do not usually do so. It was helpful if such singing continued after a child was born and if before that 'there was music in the environment from the sixth month of prenatal life, with specific moments dedicated to singing and listening, in a family atmosphere of encouragement and praise'.

First words

The first time a child very obviously uses a word will be of enormous importance in a family. For children who have a hearing impairment, a communication disorder or learning difficulty, this may be their first use of sign language such as British Sign Language. Words or signs are symbols. They stand for something else, and are imbued with meaning. The words 'Mum' or 'Dad' are not the actual people. They stand for the person, who may or may not be present. There are simpler systems for children for whom this is too abstract, such as Maketon, using a picture exchange system, or the Objects of Reference, developed by Adam Ockelford (2008).

When a child begins to use words and phrases, symbolic thinking has opened up to that child who can then think about the past, present and future, and describe and comment on events and people, expressing their thoughts and feelings and developing ideas. Marian Whitehead (2009: 10) emphasized that the first word will be used spontaneously by children. It will also be used consistently and regularly in the same context and the same activity. The parent or carer will then be able to notice it.

Pretend play scenarios

Some researchers argue that language and other kinds of symbolic behaviours are separate systems. Others would argue there are different kinds of symbolic behaviour. You will find by reading this book that the important thing is to value both the early beginnings and the later developments of symbolic behaviour, such as pretend play, drawings and paintings, models, sculptures, dance choreography, musical composition and dramatic play scenarios. The pioneering Italian educator Malaguzzi (1998) described these as 'the hundred languages of the child'. We open up a rich world for children when we help them to be symbol users and makers of their own symbols. But we need to remember the warning that relates to our use of the brain: 'Use it, or lose it'.

In order for young children to (later) be able to read and write independently, these are the essentials of literacy

Literacy has its beginnings in communication and language. Here the adult and child share a story they have made together about a train's journey. The adult tries to tune into the child's ideas, and to follow, while offering vocabulary as the play scenario develops, such as 'train engine', 'carriage', 'track'

Relating to others

- Literacy has its beginnings in social relationships, movement and the senses, communication and language.
- The way that the hands, eyes and ears co-ordinate and work together is fundamentally important both in tracking, and in the development of, phonological awareness in terms of later following print on a page, gaining pencil control, and linking sounds and letters. Children who are stacked in a certain type of pushchair will only be able to see out if their head is turned to the side. This does not support these important aspects of development.
- People need to talk with and listen to babies and young children.
- Eye contact with babies is important, and so is looking away when a baby has had enough interacting for the moment. Doing this is a problem with front-facing pushchairs or stacking pushchairs.
- Silences and pauses are also important. Adults will tend to fill such silences, when it might be important to leave these as moments of reflection and connection.
- Mirroring, turn-taking and imitation are all important in developing non-verbal and verbal conversations.

The importance of movement

- As babies crawl, their eyes must move in co-ordinated ways which will later on track text on a page (see Greenland, 2006; Bruce, Meggitt and Grenier, 2010).
- Children need to be able to co-ordinate their movements, both large (gross motor) and small (fine motor). The way in which eyes, hands, and fingers move together is vital. Arms and shoulders are also an important aspect of this. Because of the way the physical body develops, the first parts of the spine to become well co-ordinated will be the head and hands. Then the legs will do the same and walking will begin. The arms and legs start to work together. You will see in different chapters of this book that dancing, movement and action songs encourage and support the kinds of physical co-ordination needed to read and write. Unco-ordinated children will have great difficulty later on when they come to reading and writing.

Becoming a symbol maker and a symbol user

- Symbols stand for other things and people, both present and absent.
- Personal symbols hold meaning for the child because they are made by that child.
- Texts themselves (the written words) have no meaning. They represent the meanings that are rooted in personal symbols and personal experiences.
- We need to help children develop the essentials of communicating without words. (There is a whole literature, for example, on picture books: see Baddeley and Eddershaw, 1994; Styles and Bearne, 2003; Whitehead, 2007: 46–7, 99–100.)
- We need to help children make and use their own personal symbols, relating to their culture and the wider world.
- Music, dance, all the art forms, and an appreciation of literature make a huge contribution to the way children develop their understanding and become competent in reading. These give meaningful experiences of rhythm, sequence and narrative, tone and intonation, pauses, rhyme, and alliteration.
- Order (syntax), sequence and narrative help children to make meaning of texts in stories and poems, to compose their own (fiction and non-fiction), and to understand sentences, beginnings and endings.

Picture books are important for focussing children on books. The best of these will provide a subtext, so that several things are happening at the same time. Children love to find out these details, just as with life where more than one thing will occur simultaneously. This encourages them to be observant of detail, which will help when reading and writing words later on

The importance of play

Children's spontaneous free-flow play (Bruce, 1991) presents opportunities for using connecting language, for experimenting with narrative and characters, revisiting songs and rhymes and stories, making alternatives, using familiar rhymes, rhythms and alliteration, and collaborating with others in order to work as a team and bring about a satisfying play scenario. There is no prescribed script in free-flow play – rather this works in the same way as a jazz, drama or dance improvisation.

The importance of conversations with children

- Allow for repeating back, clarifying, and expanding on what children say will help language to develop.
- Using spoken language and the kind of listening that understands what is said, acts on what is said, and responds and initiates, questions and problem-solves, will ensure shared sustained conversations (Siraj-Blatchford, 2006).
- These use and understand language or signing for our own thoughts, ideas, feelings and relationships.
- These use and understand language or signing in order to talk with and respond to other people in all sorts of different situations.

Play scenario in a café. The practitioner observed the children trying to make a café, and so she helped them to gather props. She wrote 'Café' on the shopfront for them, but did not take over. She tried to support their ideas, and joined in with that in mind. The play started to flow, with customers and staff taking their characters, and 'café-type language' being used. The practitioner gave children the words they needed during the play, such as pretending to be a customer, and asking for the 'bill' or to see the 'menu', being ready to give her 'order', and wanting a 'starter' and a 'main course' as well as 'dessert'. She thought it 'cheap/expensive'.

- Children need to be able to understand what is involved in communication without words or sign language. They will not grasp the importance of a question mark if they have not captured the tone and tune of the voice when a question is asked. The sounds and subtle messages of non-verbal communications are to do with pauses; the music of anger; lovingly and affectionately muttered sounds; surprise; fear; protective shouts; a sudden look; meeting someone's gaze or avoiding eye contact; pulling someone towards us to look and share a focus; pointing … Looking and listening, as you will realize in this book, are important co-ordinations in the brain. Later on, when children read and write, the look of sentences, words and letters will need to co-ordinate with the sound of these in sophisticated ways that have become internalized processes in tracking, decoding print, and encoding the written symbols.

The importance of sounds and listening to them, especially the sounds of languages

- The sounds in words must be distinguished from one another. These are later on mapped onto the letters on the page, and the meaning must be there.

- Children need to develop and learn spoken or signed language. Many children throughout the world will speak two or three languages. Some will be lucky enough to speak three languages with entirely different roots and structures (for example, Italian, English and Urdu). This means it is relatively easy to learn any language with ease. Monolinguals who have become cut off from the music, phonology (sounds in the language) and forms of all but their own language will find this more difficult. The work of Usha Goswami (in Goouch and Lambirth, 2007) is of great value when exploring these issues.

Shared sustained conversation leads to deep thoughts – but adults can never predict when these might begin. When they do happen the important thing is to seize the moment. Conversations of this kind go beyond just describing things. They analyse how things happen, why, and what might happen next (prediction). They are about cause and effect. The adult tries to tune into the child's ideas and to expand these by describing them further and introducing cause and effect relationships: 'Why?', 'How are these important?', 'What next do you think?'

Rhythm, rhyme, intonation, alliteration

- Phonological awareness (the ability to distinguish between similar and different sounds in the language) is crucial to later reading and writing. It is helped when children can hear the differences between phonemes, syllables, initial sounds and rhyming chunks. (These terms are all discussed in later chapters of the book.) Usha Goswami (in Goouch and Lambirth, 2007) has collected data across languages which point to the development of phonological awareness following a similar sequence. Children gain awareness of syllables first, then rhyming chunks, and eventually – and only through direct teaching – phonemes.
- Rhythm (music, dance and song) helps children with syllabification, blending and segmentation.
- Tone, intonation and pauses in the language help children to understand punctuation.

Distinguishing sounds. Using musical instruments is one way of helping children to distinguish between one sound and another. Experiencing the sounds that everyday objects make is another. 'Is this a loud or quiet sound/A long or short sound?', 'It is a high or low sound?', 'Which is louder? Longer? Lower?', 'Which is your favourite?'

The boys readily listen to the sounds when rhymes are with action and props. Young children find it difficult to listen to sounds without a context, because they become isolated from meaningful experience. Unless learning carries personal meaning, it does not become embedded or connected to the rest of learning. Margaret Donaldson (1978) suggests that this is the difference between embedded and disembedded learning and thinking

- Rhyme helps children to hear patterns and distinguish between those that sound similar and different, as well as to see patterns which help them to decode and encode words as they read and write.
- Alliteration helps children to hear repetition of the smallest units of sound (phonemes) and to see the smallest units of sound in print (graphemes) at the beginning of words.

Time-honoured traditions

- Baby songs, action songs sitting on the spot and later moving from the spot, nursery rhymes both traditional and modern, and carefully introduced poetry cards help children to put all of this together.
- Action songs help the co-ordination of sound, vision and body movements. They can be on the spot with upper body movements. They can be moving about using co-ordinated arm and leg movements. All of this is important for later reading and writing co-ordination of the senses (including hearing and vision) and the physical body.
- Nursery rhymes and stories help a sense of narrative, storyline and characters, and in creating events and contexts and new worlds, alternative worlds, imaginative worlds. They can help children to engage in 'connecting language' ('and', 'but', 'then', 'before', 'after', 'soon') (Ragnarsdottir, 2006). They can encourage oral and aural blending and segmenting (more of these terms later) – aspects of later reading and writing.
- Poetry cards can give children opportunities to engage with small, manageable chunks of text in order to learn about the alphabetic principle and also to explore how sounds will map onto graphemes (letters or clusters of letters in a word).

High well-being

- Ensure the child has high well-being, and is confident enough to problem-solve their way into reading and writing, to have a go, predict, confirm and self-correct. Both beginners and independent readers need to do this. This is very different from guessing.
- Introduce the essentials of literacy at a pace that is comfortable for each child.

- Support and extend a child's literacy learning in the right way for him or her, at the right time, with that child's full and willing engagement.
- Set children on the path to becoming life-long readers and writers for pleasure, information and understanding from the start, by enjoying music, song and dance and by sharing books, rhymes and poetry.

The essentials of literacy make it possible for children to:

- read and write using print or Braille
- open up worlds of literature
- open up worlds of knowledge and information
- open up worlds to inhabit through creative writing
- connect with the thoughts, feelings and relationships of others
- connect with both their cultures and those of others.

Diversity and inclusion

For very good reasons not all children will speak in words, read or write (owing to having complex needs or learning difficulties), but when this is so, they will need to be able to communicate, with or without language or signs. Children enjoy books, drama, music and dance experiences that are found in stories and poems. They may be the kind of personality that prefers and gains pleasure from information books and the experiences of nature and everyday life that go with this. The journey into literacy is complex, and cannot be normalized or standardized. One size does not fit all. Although human beings are social beings, they are not herds to be driven.

The nursery rhyme 'Incy Wincy Spider' is chanted while using the props. It is easier to learn long sentences in songs than it is to repeat a long sentence in ordinary talking because the music gives the words a shape through the rhythms, and helps to bring some order and pattern to the language. Having props and actions gives further support and brings the words alive, as can be seen in the photograph

'Five Currant Buns in a Baker's Shop' – there is evident enjoyment here. When children are learning in a relaxed and unpressured atmosphere they open up to learning and become engaged in the process. They also show more initiative and are pro-active learners

How to avoid undermining the essentials of literacy

- Encourage **crawling** on the floor.
- Encourage the use of **face-to-face pushchairs**, which will give adult and child a shared focus (looking at the same things together), and talking about what you both can see, hear, smell.
- Avoid pushchairs which stack children so the one underneath cannot look ahead, and can only have a partial view that involves looking to one side or the other.
- Discourage the use of mobile phones on outings and, instead, engage in **talking with** (not at) babies, toddlers and young children.
- Over-use of dummies constrains language development. These can, however, help children with consistently blocked tubes to clear these and be less nasal, hear and sleep better, and to be more relaxed and open to learning.
- Do not rush children into formal instruction in reading and writing. Build their language development with a rich vocabulary and encourage them to express their ideas, thoughts and feelings, and talk about their relationships with people, animals, nature, stories and so on. Reading and writing rest on the firm foundation of language development.

TAKING TRADITIONAL PRACTICE FORWARD IN A LEARNING COMMUNITY

In the chapters that follow, we shall be looking at some traditional ways in which practitioners and parents across the centuries have very effectively and successfully helped babies, toddlers and children to become:

- effective communicators (spoken and unspoken)
- avid bookworms, mark-makers and writers
- readers, at the right time and in the right way for individual children
- seekers of knowledge, understanding and information by a sensitive tuning-in with others, discussion, reading and writing
- appreciators of literature
- on the path to becoming enthusiastic and committed readers and writers for the rest of their lives.

First, we shall look at what is meant by enabling literacy environments indoors and outdoors.

KEY TERMS

Phonological awareness – children need to be able to notice, identify and use the different sounds that make up words. They need to be able to do this in different ways. Psycholinguistic 'Grain sizes' are big, middle, and small (see Goswami, in Goouch and Lambirth, 2007)

- Big – **syllables** – In the word 'dinosaur' (a much-loved word for young children) the syllables are: di–no–saur
- Middle – **rhyming chunks** – In the word 'love' (another word much-loved by young children), when hearing the difference between **l**ove and **d**ove, the last part of each word rhymes but the beginnings sound different. These are sometimes called **onset-rimes**
- Small – **phonemes** – In order to read and write, children begin to be able to identify the phonemes they hear in words. As language develops they begin to do this gradually, and they need direct adult help to do so. This need for direct teaching, Ziegler and Goswami (2006) suggest, is not surprising because the phoneme is not a natural speech unit. It is best developed through singing and dancing together with rhymes, poems and much-loved and quoted phrases in stories. The word 'bike', much used by children, has three phonemes: b-i-ke

Phonemic awareness – **graphemes and phonemes working together.** When children are becoming phonologically aware, they begin to be able to make links between the way the smallest units of speech sound, and the way they look (the graphemes) when they are written down. Making the link between the smallest sounds and the smallest units of writing (the letters) seems to be central to learning to read and write. As Goswami (in Goouch and Lambirth, 2007: 127) says, 'Letters are used to symbolise phonemes'

Reading

Bayley, R. (2007) *Action Raps*. Birmingham: Lawrence Educational.

A Treasure-chest of Lullabies and Songs from Southwark parents suitable for all young children (booklet and CD). (Supported by Every Child a Talker (ECAT) Project, 2010, and published by In the Picture – available from inthepicture.info)

Further Reading

Whitehead, M. (2010) *Language and Literacy in the Early Years 0–7* (4th edn). London: SAGE.

Chapter 2

Observing Children in an Enabling Environment

In this chapter we show how:

- careful observation enables practitioners to know each child in order to support the individual's journey into literacy;
- the practitioner supports an individual child's needs and pace of learning;
- practitioners can create an enabling environment that will respond to a child's needs.

Observing children

Effective observation informs the way in which we work with children and their families: 'Records are about getting to know the child and what the child needs' (Bartholomew and Bruce, 1993: 100); 'The impact of observational assessment is not measurable by its weight. It is the use to which the practitioner puts their observations that is important' (*Creating the Picture*, 2007: 8).

Observation helps us to

- find the child's voice through their interests and needs
- track a child's development and learning
- plan for the child in appropriate ways
- keep in mind the whole child

- use everyday situations to assess the child's progress
- work with parents
- work with other professionals
- see the child in different situations across time.

Making a narrative observation

Systems need to be in place so that every child is observed regularly and these observations are shared with parents who are then encouraged to contribute. Narrative observations tell a story about a child's interests and needs. They are also part of a formative assessment. When observing:

- Note the time of day and the date, and the child's age.
- Write briefly about the context of the observation. Indoors? Outdoors? In the sandpit? Eating lunch?
- Write down as exact a description as possible of what the child says and does. If other children are also involved, write down a suitably long description of the conversations and actions of other children to give a clear picture of the observed child.
- Do not write judgementally.
- Ensure the observation can be analysed and interpreted afterwards.
- Make sure the observation can be linked with observations of the child made by other people (including parents).
- Ensure the observations can inform any planning.

Making an anecdotal observation

Not all observations will be on-the-spot, narrative observations. Some will be anecdotal. This means the practitioner has remembered back and noted something afterwards. It is a good idea to use a different coloured pen for narrative observations (perhaps a black one) and anecdotal observations (say a blue one). Stick-on notes will often be handy to make this kind of observation.

It is important to find useful lenses through which to analyse observations

There are many different lenses through which to analyse the observations and each of these will be useful in different situations and for different purposes. We can use the following to help us analyse our observations:

- The Well-being Scale (Laevers, 1994);
- The Leuven Involvement Scale (Laevers, 1994): a process-orientated child monitoring system for young children ('The Leuven Scales'), Experiential Education Series no. 2, Centre for Experiential Education);
- The Child Engagement Scale (for children from birth to 3 years) (Pascal and Bertram, 2006), 'Connectedness, Exploration and Meaning Making';

- 'The Twelve Features of Play' (Bruce, 1991; updated on pages 36–7);
- The *Early Years Foundation Stage* (DfES, 2007a) areas of Development and Learning (and, in future, the reviewed form of this document) links to the official framework document of the country.

Free-flow play (Bruce, 1991) using 'See-saw Margery Daw'. This play episode started with one child, joined by another, when they then tried to sing and create a see-saw. They had had previous experience of see-saws (feature 1). They initiated and controlled their play, making up their own rules (feature 2), and they turned the plank into a play prop (feature 3). No-one made them do this; it was their own spontaneous idea (feature 4). They enjoyed playing together (feature 8) and wallowed in their play (feature 10). They used a recently acquired skill of balancing (feature 11) and this all came together as they brought to the play their knowledge of a song, see-saws, and balancing and taking turns (feature 12). The twelve features of free-flow play (Bruce, 1991) appear in an updated form later in this chapter (pages 36–7)

Children engage with their learning

Many nurseries now have children's folders that will include photographs, examples of drawings and writing, all of which are available for children and families to view whenever they would like to (Hutchins, 2006). Being part of a learning community means that the spirit is not competitive or judgemental. Instead, everyone involved is trying to build on a child's interests and needs.

The only records not open are those relating to child protection, containing sensitive data and medical records.

Multi-professional teams working in integrated ways

Practitioners from different training backgrounds will emphasize different aspects of the child's growing, developing and learning. This is invaluable. The contributions of health visitors, speech and language therapists, physiotherapists, art therapists, music therapists, psychologists and so on, all give different perspectives which can help teachers and early years practitioners to create a picture of each child.

Assessment

Each of the four countries making up the UK has a mandatory framework document for the early years. Since devolution these are becoming increasingly different in the way they are constructed. Other countries have also developed framework documents for use in a variety of settings, such as Te Whāriki in New Zealand. In Italy, the Reggio Emilia and Pistoria approaches are not mandatory, but they exert powerful influence on practice. It is important, wherever children grow up in the world, to observe and act in the light of observations, in order to support children in their journeys of communicating, developing language(s) enjoyment of books, reading for pleasure and information, and writing, for real reasons and to carry flights of the imagination.

It is important to bear in mind that assessment wags the tail of any official framework document for early childhood curriculum and pedagogy (the interface between a child's development and learning). Assessment is not the same as record-keeping. One of the problems which is in urgent need of addressing is that practitioners record too much and assess too little. Assessment is about knowing the child. It shows significant points in a child's journey through communication, language, literacy and literature which need to be shared with parents through rich dialogues. This is formative assessment, which guides practitioners and parents together so that they can help the child in their developing learning, and consider what might be helpful next. It is also necessary to pause and gather together key insights and significant markers from the journey through summative assessment.

The way assessment is structured in the English framework document is as a result of the review of the *Early Years Foundation Stage* chaired by Dame Clare Tickell, which will bring changes to the assessment process with far reaching impact.

Despite the fact that governments and their frameworks come and go, one replacing the other with increasing pace, there has, since the 1930s, been remarkable continuity in terms of what practitioners and parents emphasise as important for babies, toddlers and young children. However, there is not agreement about how this should be put into language and described. Warm, affectionate and loving relationships, emotional well-being, physical care and nurture – these resonate with the study by Parry and Archer in the 1960s. But there is less emphasis on the fulfilment reached by babies, toddlers and young children in having ideas, trying them out and developing them.

Bruner, also in the 1960s, counteracted this focus on social, emotional and physical development, arguing that any subject can be taught at any age in an intellectually honest fashion. This means that, for example, a baby who babbles 'ma, ma, ma' and is answered by his mother, and is fascinated to hear himself echoed, is at the beginning of experiencing phonemes through developing phonological awareness during development in the first few years of life. There are layers of understanding which emerge slowly and through rich experiences of language sounds.

This gradual learning presents problems for those working professionally with young babies and children. When does babble become a phoneme? Does it matter? It only matters if social, emotional and physical development are seen as context free. Relationships happen in real situations, through real experiences, such as sharing a book. Sharing a book with a baby is all about literature in an atmosphere of love and affection, physical comfortableness, and social enjoyment together. This illustrates how important it is to focus on the whole child, and the journey into knowledge of various kinds. Every aspect is important, including the intellectual life of the child. Babies and young children love to think, but they need people who help and support them in doing this in real and rich experiences of literature (fiction) and information texts (non-fiction).

Continuing the learning journey: moving to a school where there is good early years practice until children are seven years old

Play props for 'Five Freckled Frogs' (or is it six?). The child on the right counted the frogs, but said there were six. She looked again, as if she instinctively felt this was not what she expected. The next time she pointed at each frog. There were six. She knew the song about five little frogs and took one of the frogs away. Then she counted again, pointing at each frog, and the answer was five. She smiled. Pointing by the child (not someone pointing on the child's behalf) seems to help children to follow print or count objects

- *Transitions* Transitions are important. Good transitions mean there is no loss of learning. Bad transitions mean unhappy children, or children who will become unsteady in their learning while they adjust to a new life. The first transition is from the home to a childminder or a group setting.
- *Moving together with friends* Groups of children who move together, from an early childhood setting into a school, seem to achieve better. They have established relationships with other children that can ease the transition and enable them to learn more effectively.

Children flourish where good early years practice is in place from birth to seven years with a seamless progression. Marian Whitehead (2007: 79–93) writes about what makes up an enabling environment in communication, language and literacy for children up to eight years old.

When we are working with children we need to look out for key moments in order to record their progress in a wide range of different aspects of communication, language, and a love of literature as displayed in fiction and non-fiction reading and writing. This will show itself in their play scenarios; their interest in labels and print in the environment; how they engage with other children and adults; when and how they seek out books; how they play with language; their enjoyment of movement, music and dance; and whether they spontaneously choose to mark-make and attempt to write. As children become older, the detail of what we record needs to track their progress and the help needs to carefully match their needs, and continued engagement with literature and finding out, their seeking information and commenting on the world about them as their literacy develops.

Creating the atmosphere

We have seen that it is important for adults to be good observers of children so that they can respond in supportive ways to the things that worry, interest and fascinate children. Tuning into children means adults know how they feel, think and relate to people, and when they are in or out of their comfort zone. It allows practitioners, working in close partnership with parents and carers, to extend the developing learning in the right way and at the right time.

We saw that literacy rests on communication and linguistic development.

Tuning into children means adults know how they feel, think and relate to people, and when they are in or out of their comfort zone. It enables practitioners, working in close partnership with parents and carers, to extend the developing learning of the children they work with in ways and at times that are right for them. Here the practitioner is enjoying spending time with a boy who has been mark-making on a large sheet of paper. The silences are as important as the talking together. She makes remarks such as, 'I like the way you did a twirly bit there.' Pause. He ponders. And so it goes on

Children need to grow up in an atmosphere where there is sensitive, non-verbal communication and encouragement to put things into words (or signs). Children will talk with us readily about what they find interesting, or what they find surprising. They need explanations and reasons why they cannot do something, or should or should not have done something. They will talk with us about stories, the models they make, their drawings and dances, music, and the nature in their garden *if* they find adults are sensitive to their feelings and thoughts and are genuinely interested.

Giving children time to express their thoughts and feelings in an unrushed atmosphere means:

- Not speaking for the child.
- Talking *with* children, not *at* them.
- Having a conversation, not giving a monologue.
- Giving the child undivided attention.
- Sharing experiences together which are worthwhile.
- Making sure children feel that what they say is valued and appreciated.

The adult shows genuine interest in the conversation. She is at eye level with the child so that eye contact is easy. Her body language is showing him that she wants to communicate with him, and she listens to him without interrupting and taking over. These are non-verbal kinds of communication. These are of central importance and form a backcloth to what we say and how we listen and respond to others. There are cultural differences in the way this takes place, so that as well as speaking different languages we also move differently depending on the culture and the language spoken

- Having conversations face to face with children, not towering above them.
- Following a young child's gaze to see what they are interested in.
- When not sure what a child says, saying what we think they said.
- Or asking the child if we are right about what they said.
- Or asking the child to repeat what they said.
- Remembering that conversations are about taking turns.
- Asking questions that help conversations. What now? What if? How does this work?
- Avoiding conversation-stoppers by demanding replies, such as when adults ask a question that they already know the answer to, but insist the child answers.
- Finding out what interests the child, as they will be more likely to want to talk about their interests.

Conversations

With babies and toddlers we will try to match our actions and what we say with the child's. This echoing, side-by-side behaviour is an important part of communication.

Another important strategy is to rephrase with correct grammar what the child has said. For example, 'I goed out' can be rephrased as 'You did go out didn't you?'

When we chat with children, it is important that we have shared, sustained conversations (REPEY, 2002). We need to do this by expanding on what the child says. For example, if a toddler says 'Gone' we might say, 'Yes! The dog has gone hasn't he?' Helping children to talk so they go beyond the here and now is important too: i.e. what we did, where we will go.

It is important to remember that children with disabilities and complex needs may not be able to take part in shared, sustained conversations that use spoken words. Sign language, Maketon or Picture Exchange Communication System (PECS) might be more appropriate. For some children Objects of Reference, developed by Professor Adam Ockelford (2008), may be a good way forward for developing communication.

British Sign Language is mostly used by deaf people. It has a grammar and is officially designated as a language, but instead of using spoken words it uses signs. As with any other language it is always evolving and has regional and country variations. Those using BSL in the north of England will create a slightly different usage to those in the south, for example. There are also differences between American Sign Language (ASL) and British Sign language (BSL).

Maketon has a list of over 400 items with a corresponding sign or symbol. These symbols are based on BSL but they are used to support spoken English. Because the signs rely on positions, movements and facial positions, they cannot be learnt from the manual. It is important for parents and practitioners to learn together with the child. The Maketon Project offers support to those who are learning Maketon.

PECS teaches children to exchange a picture for the desired item with an adult who will at once respond to the request. For example, if a child would like a drink he or she will give the adult the picture of a cup and the adult will give them a drink. The adult does not use verbal prompts and so the child is encouraged to be spontaneous. Children go on to construct sentences, and are helped to ask and answer questions, or to make comments about experiences. This is a very useful system to use with children who have autism, for example.

Objects of Reference is a personalised set of objects gathered together for a particular child. These help children who are challenged in developing language to learn about, for example, the sequence of the day. This is because each object is symbolic. The small drum might mean that there will be a music session. Then after that the cup means it will be snack time. This helps a child to predict and get a sense of the shape of the day.

Children readily engage with pleasure and fascination with accents, dialects, rhymes and creoles. All this helps them to work out what is involved in language and literacy, and literature. The diversity of the UK today greatly enhances this possibility. In the main accents are about variations in pronunciation. We would talk about Yorkshire and Dorset accents in England, for example. Dialects however are variations on a language, based on a community or region. Children who speak a dialect of English are often thought to speak ungrammatically, and

Matching pictures and words. Traditionally, children have always enjoyed games of matching and sorting. Pictures and words help children to make connections between different kinds of symbolic representation. The written word 'cat' is different from a picture of a cat. Malaguzzi, the Italian educator who worked in Reggio Emilia, emphasized the importance of the 'hundred languages of the child'. Symbolic representations express what he meant by this

they can be misunderstood if this is the case. Creole languages develop when several languages come together, and bits of each are taken into what will become a new language. They often develop when people who speak different languages come together to live in close communities and to work together. They need to communicate and therefore they use their own language and pick up phrases and words from their neighbours' language – thus it turns into a creole.

Play with language and its sounds

Nonsense words that rhyme

Children, as we noted earlier, delight in playing with the sounds and words of their language. They readily make up nonsense words and particularly enjoy making rhyming strings.

Matching pictures and words

Children build up a sight vocabulary, matching words and pictures in games. This helps later on with word recognition.

Voice sounds

These often happen quite spontaneously. When Sam saw and smelt rotten food that was nine days old, he uttered a disgusted sound – 'Errrrh!' These are moments to capture, as the practitioner here did, because she wrote it down. In this way, children begin to use long and short vowel sounds, which will be important as they learn to read.

The (hidden) importance of play

Play opens up the world of literacy in ways that are appropriate and right for young children. Children who do not have opportunities for play with narrative and story-making, with characters and creating places and events, will often *appear* to be making sufficient progress in their reading and writing at Key Stage 1. Hrafnhildur Ragnarsdottir (2006) and her colleagues in Iceland and Norway have argued that their research is beginning to show that poorly developing narrative and discourse (connected language) proficiency does not show up on word recognition and word comprehension tests until children are about nine years old. These children will have great difficulty with reading comprehension. This is important because it may be thought that testing children on a word recognition list that includes nonsense words can assess their progress in reading at six or seven years of age. In fact it is opposite and Ragnarsdottir and colleagues have shown this.

Why narrative (stories, poems and rhymes) supports later word recognition and word comprehension

Children who do not have a good grasp of all these essentials of literacy will have difficulty in reading comprehension and writing, but this does not become obvious until they are about nine years old according to Ragnarsdottir. Dominic Wyse (2008) also emphasizes a rich literature environment, full of stories and poetry and rhymes. He has written very rigorous and thorough critiques of narrow approaches to the teaching of reading, based only on synthetic phonics introduced early (first, fast and only).

Ragnarsdottir (2006) emphasizes the importance of the narrative:

In their play, and through being introduced to rich stories and poems and rhymes in a traditional as well as current range of literature, children will develop the essentials of literacy they will need later on for their reading comprehension and recognition. Nursery rhymes give children very simple experiences of narrative. Humpty sits on a wall, has a fall, and cannot be put back together again

- in the literature (stories, poetry, rhymes) we tell and read to children, and it is worthwhile to get them to act out, and re-enact, with small world, dressing-up clothes and so on;
- in the spontaneous free-flow play of children, when they make the storyline and the characters who live out the stories they create, as these are often based around the stories we have told them, or the television and digital versatile disk (DVD) material they have seen at home.

Listening to and making narratives with stories and characters has a long-term impact on vocabulary development and discourse proficiency (the way children connect the words) in young children. According to Ragnarsdottir, there are essential elements for a child's journey into literacy:

- understanding narrative, and having a storyline with characters
- developing a rich vocabulary, which is important for reading and writing
- connecting words; linking different ideas, different places and times; referring back and forward to events; setting the scene and making characters; being clear enough for the listener to understand; showing characters' inner feelings; recounting a series of events
- sequencing events in a story
- acting out a story
- being clear enough for the listener to understand the story when retelling a story (this is called theory of mind – being on the inside of what it is like to be listening to the story and what information that person needs)

- thinking about how to make the listener feel suspense, or feel that the story is convincing
- having enough vocabulary to tell the story
- developing your own 'voice' in telling the story
- developing phonological awareness
- using connectors to join words with increasing complexity
- setting the scene for the story ('and', 'the', 'but', 'here', 'there', 'this one', 'although')
- establishing the characters and introducing them to the listener

- having a starting-point for the story
- developing a storyline or plot
- resolving the story with an ending
- using direct speech from the characters in role
- using characters who see things from different points of view.

Jumping off Humpty's wall

All these elements develop through the free-flow play of children and are hugely helpful, these researchers argue, for their later skill in creative and factual writing as well as for their reading comprehension and recognition. They also argue that if these are not in place by about nine years of age, children are likely to display low scores in literacy and other school work.

The features of free-flow play (Bruce, 1991, updated here)

One of the ways practitioners can become informed about children's play is through reflecting on the features of play as it flows.

There are 12 features of play which help practitioners to see a child's developing learning:

Free-flow play (Bruce, 1991) with Humpty Dumpty. This uses first-hand experience, making up rules, finding props, choosing to play, playing together, owning the play, engaged, showing physical competence, integrating thoughts and feelings around Humpty Dumpty. This is probably not pretending, or rehearsing the future. Nine out of 12 features of play are present. This is rich, free-flow play

- Look out for the way children use the first-hand experiences they have had.
- Note how children stay in control as they play, making up their own rules in order to do so.
- Look at how children make or find play props.

- Children cannot be made to play. They choose to play and cannot do this to order. They also choose to join others in play, or to initiate play spontaneously.
- Children rehearse the future as they create role play and possible scenarios.
- Play might involve pretending.
- Children might choose to play alone.
- Children and children, or children and adults, might play together, either in parallel or co-operatively in pairs or groups.
- Every player will have his or her own personal play agenda, although he or she may not be aware of it!
- Rich play means that a child will be deeply engaged, difficult to distract, and wallowing in what they are doing.
- Children try out their latest learning, skills and competencies as they play. Play is not so much about learning new things as celebrating new learning.
- As children play, they co-ordinate their ideas, feelings and thoughts, and they make sense of their relationships with family, friends and the culture(s) in which they are growing up. Play that is integrated in these ways flows in a sustained way, which is why it is called free-flow play (Bruce, 1991, updated here).

The organic garden is an important part of the enabling environment, and while she tends the plants the little girl sings 'Mary, Mary, quite contrary, how does your garden grow?' The richer the experiences children have, the more they are able to make links with stories and songs and nursery rhymes. This helps children to engage with literature

Revisiting rhymes is important. One of the findings of research on eye movements (Rayner, Juhasz and Pollatsek in Snowling and Hume, 2007) during reading shows that it is not just a case of physically looking at a word (fixating) and moving along the text (saccades). The thinking a reader does influences how the eyes move, and the richer the child's vocabulary, and the more the child can predict the words of the text, the better. It also means the child does not have to fixate for so long on a word, and that helps the flow of the reading which keeps the meaning central.

Revisiting rhymes

Reading without meaning is soul destroying and a depressing thing to do. Young children should not be subjected to this. It will put them off reading.

Props boxes to support the stories and rhymes

Gathering materials to be stored in a box, so that children can spontaneously create a whole scenario, opens up the possibility to act and retell, and to make variations on the theme in play. This is offered by the adult who puts together the box. Boxes are invaluable and often stored on a high shelf, which means these can be brought down as needed and will fit the planning if based on an observation of children's interests and needs.

Dressing-up clothes to support stories and rhymes

These should not be expensive and commercially made and bought from catalogues. There are two kinds of people. Some will prefer to dress exactly like a character and will go to endless trouble making and gathering the relevant clothes. Four-year-olds often want realism. Others will use dressing-up clothes as a suggestion only which will signal the character they are going to turn into.

Acting out rhymes in real situations

To sing 'Mary, Mary Quite Contrary' in the garden, and to grow flowers that are bell shaped (like bluebells and lily of the valley) and place shells along the edges, brings the song alive. The vocabulary can then be remembered easily, which will help a later reading of the rhyme when it is written down.

Role play

Pretending to be a nurse, or a postperson, a shopkeeper or a car mechanic helps children to develop a sense of character and to weave a story. These are hugely important elements of reading and writing – story and character – and they are especially valuable later on when children are developing their creative writing.

Children spontaneously and creatively making their own props and using them as they sing songs and rhymes or retell stories

Children who are encouraged to make their own props are more likely to engage with developing the story characters they have met in books and rhymes and to make their own characters, often using these for inspiration (Meek et al., 1977). They will then begin to tell and gradually to play and write their own stories.

Sharing books together, as well as looking at books alone

Children benefit from having a book corner, which needs to be warm, light and cosy. Cushions on the floor cater for those who like lounging with books. In addition a small table and chairs will be more comfortable for other children, while

'Dr Foster went to Gloucester/In a shower of rain/He stepped in a puddle/Right up to his middle/And never went there again.' The important thing about this rhyme is that the words rhyme, but when they are written down they look quite different. It is therefore best to enjoy singing this rhyme with children, and not to spend time asking them to look at the written form. Some nursery rhymes are more useful for their rhyming and rhythm, and less useful as early texts to be read, as is the case here

'Rain, rain go away/Come again another day.' The rhythm is important here, and so is the rhyming chunk. Rain is repeated, so this makes it easy to recognize when the rhyme is written down. 'Away' rhymes with 'day'. The rhyming chunk is 'ay' and the beginnings are different – 'aw' and 'd'

some may also appreciate a sofa so they can be cosy as they share books together with adults.

Children need to be able to choose books to look at and become absorbed in, or to share with an adult and perhaps one other child. This re-creates the feeling of a bedtime story (Brice-Heath, 1983). It is a relaxed atmosphere, and a child can create a dialogue around the text and story or the rhyme in a book.

There should be a good range of books covering poetry and rhymes, stories and non-fiction. Those with both music and songs are very popular while books made by practitioners with and for children are usually much loved by parents and children.

Sharing a book. It is important that the practitioner is sitting down and at the children's level. She has a small group so that there is a feeling of cosiness which in turn makes a relaxed atmosphere. Children should not be made to feel rushed, and the adult's attention should not wander. Any interruption of this time together should be discouraged

When displays are taken down, practitioners will often put these into home-made books for the book corner, where everyone will be able to take trips down memory lane about the experiences they have shared together.

Book boxes

A practitioner in a pre-school playgroup said the following:

We have always had a wide range of books. We have altered our book corner to extend it with a listening corner, and our writing corner, where children have free access to a wide range of mark-making resources. We have purchased more books, big and small, both fiction and non-fiction, to relate to current topics and children's own interests. We have offered books to borrow which has been a success.

Borrowing books

Having a system in place so that children and their families can take books home to enjoy is becoming widespread practice. Older brothers and sisters will often enjoy reading to their younger siblings. This is invaluable when children need simple texts which they might be embarrassed to choose for themselves, but this allows them to do so in a relaxed way if they are reading for a younger child.

Older children reading to younger children

Many schools have special times in the week when older children can enjoy coming into the nursery to share books with younger children. This is especially valuable in supporting children to read more fluently and with greater confidence. It also encourages children to read with expression. If they do not, the younger child will quickly lose interest. This means that it keeps the reasons for reading at the centre. Without meaning, reading print is pointless for everyone.

Children benefit from being with children who are a few steps ahead of them in their literacy journeys. It helps them to see what is involved, and encourages rehearsal, or seeking help when they need it. Mixed-age groups give rich opportunities for this to happen. Two-year-olds will often imitate writing and reading behaviour when they see their three- and four-year-old friends engaging in representational drawings, or writing their names, or the approximate reading of a rhyme (Matthews, 2003).

Listening corner

Sometimes children will want to listen on their own to a story. They will not yet have reached the point where they can read it for themselves, but they have still become aware of the fact that print carries meaning and can be read. This takes away the frustration for beginner readers if they can hear a story read on a tape and turn the pages of the book as they follow it. Rhymes are a good way of giving children manageable chunks of text for this purpose. Children often point to the print as they hear the words, and engage in 'approximate' reading as their finger starts at the beginning and ends at the end, but gets a bit lost in the middle. This helps children to understand the importance of following sentences in a text.

The importance of fiction

Stories, poetry and rhyme are time-honoured ways in which children are introduced to culture. Sometimes we tell stories, poems or rhymes without using books. Sometimes we will use books. The oral tradition is more powerful in some cultures than others, but where it is strong there is usually a greater participation by people in dance, song, music and drama. Story books need to draw children in when we read to them, but as Margaret Donaldson (1978) suggests, children have not often met an author and so they are more remote to them. Children need both aspects.

Short stories

Sayings

Marian Whitehead (2007: 33) sees 'sayings' as a shared shorthand which people have said, often for centuries, and passed on using word of mouth. Tom (aged two years and six months) was at the top of the stairs with his mother and her friend. His mother said, 'I smell a rat.' He started to sniff the air, and went all the way down the stairs, saying, 'I can't smell a rat, Mummy.' This is an example of how a young child works out what is a real statement and what is a saying.

An adult may say to a child trying to zip up his coat, 'Can I help you? We can do it

Stories, poetry and rhyme are time-honoured ways by which children are introduced to culture

Nursery rhymes give children some of the essentials of literacy in a simple form. They should never be used in isolation but as part of a rich backcloth of play and first-hand experiences both indoors and outdoors, and interconnected with every area of development and learning. They can be presented in books, on cards, with small world props, through dressing-up clothes and acting out, and through the provision of play props

'Approximate reading' of a favourite rhyme. It is not a good idea for an adult to point and ask a child to read a rhyme. But it can be very helpful to a child if they are encouraged to point at the text themselves. In this way children will often begin to match this, pointing to each word, and to realize that the words we say can be connected to what we see on the page. They will often look thrilled when their finger arrives at the end of the line of text at the same time as what they say ends!

between us. Where there's a will there's a way.' Understanding sayings is part of our linguistic development.

Rhymes and poems

As Opie and Opie (1988) have shown, nursery rhymes and singing games give children important messages about the history of a culture, and open up opportunities to talk about how things have changed. They provide short chunks of phrases, which children will enjoy for their alliteration and rhyme patterns. An example would be 'Ring a Ring o' Roses'. This refers to plague, perhaps referring back to contagion in the 1390s as well as in 1665. The roses were the boils on the skin, and the posies were the herbs carried to hide the smell of sickness and were thought to ward off contagion. One saying that goes with this is:

1665, not a soul alive.
1666, London burnt to sticks.

Longer stories

Folk tales, myths and legends

It would take another book to do justice to the longer stories we tell children. Folk tales from all over the world provide a rich form of story telling, oral in their origins but now written down and presented with beautiful illustrations for children. Favourite folk tales would include *Anansi, The Enormous Turnip, Chicken Licken, The Little Red Hen, The Gingerbread Man* and *Babushka*. Favourite myths and legends might also include the story of King Midas. Margaret Meek has been relentless in emphasizing and reminding practitioners and politicians dictating educational policy that *what* children read is of central importance. The content of the literature and information books we offer to children should be the best quality possible. No one, adult or child, wants to put their effort into reading something boring, pointless, or of no use or beauty to try to deepen their understanding and knowledge about feelings, relationships, thoughts and ideas.

Everyday stories

Children engage with stories about going to see Gran, going to the shops, making bread rolls, or getting wet in the rain. The best of these kinds of stories are often those where practitioners have made books for children based around particular shared experiences they have had.

Information books

It is often observed that there is a tendency for boys (Whitehead, 2010: 172) to enjoy looking at non-fiction, information books more than stories. It is therefore very important to have a good balance of fiction and non-fiction books.

Humpty Dumpty play. The horses and the king's men are wearing simple dressing-up clothes made by the practitioners and offered to the children. There was no pressure to participate, but this proved a very popular nursery rhyme

Non-fiction books to support every part of the enabling environment both indoors and outdoors

The book corner is of central importance, but it is also very important to have books everywhere. This can easily become clutter. It is therefore important to match books to the learning environment both indoors and outdoors.

Fiction books with play props

Dressing-up clothes and play props can often prove a bit random. But if stories become much-loved favourites, children appreciate having the relevant materials to create play scenarios around them. These will often make variations on a theme (Bruce, 2004a).

The richest play will emerge if children can create their own play props. Having cloaks, a few scarves and hats, basic tunics and open-ended props can trigger and suggest ideas to children (Bruce, 2001).

The use of props with rhymes and songs and stories

The possibilities here are endless, and a source of rich experiences in communication, language and literacy. They open up the worlds of drama, music, song and dance as well as literature.

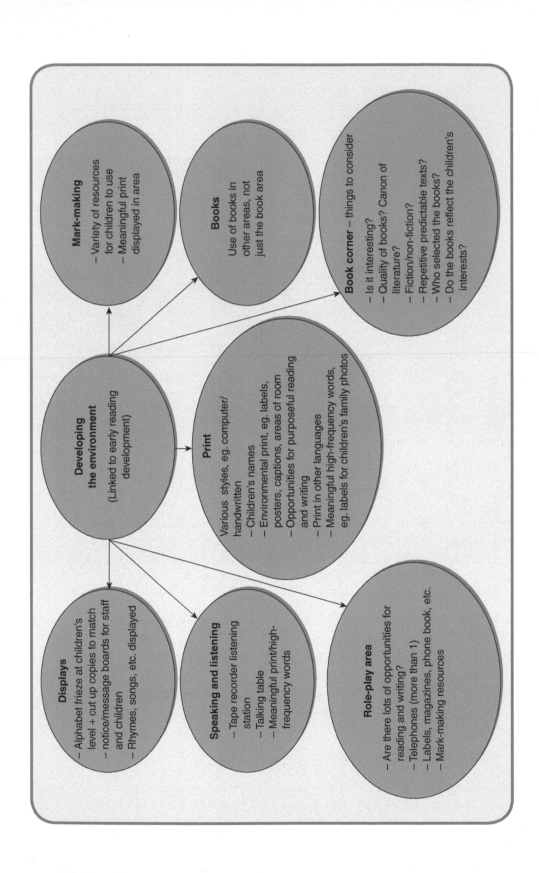

Developing the environment

(Linked to early reading development)

Mark-making
– Variety of resources for children to use
– Meaningful print displayed in area

Books
Use of books in other areas, not just the book area

Book corner – things to consider
– Is it interesting?
– Quality of books? Canon of literature?
– Fiction/non-fiction?
– Repetitive predictable texts?
– Who selected the books?
– Do the books reflect the children's interests?

Print
Various styles, eg. computer/handwritten
– Children's names
– Environmental print, eg. labels, posters, captions, areas of room
– Opportunities for purposeful reading and writing
– Print in other languages
– Meaningful high-frequency words, eg. labels for children's family photos

Displays
– Alphabet frieze at children's level + cut up copies to match
– notice/message boards for staff and children
– Rhymes, songs, etc. displayed

Speaking and listening
– Tape recorder listening station
– Talking table
– Meaningful print/high-frequency words

Role-play area
– Are there lots of opportunities for reading and writing?
– Telephones (more than 1)
– Labels, magazines, phone book, etc.
– Mark-making resources

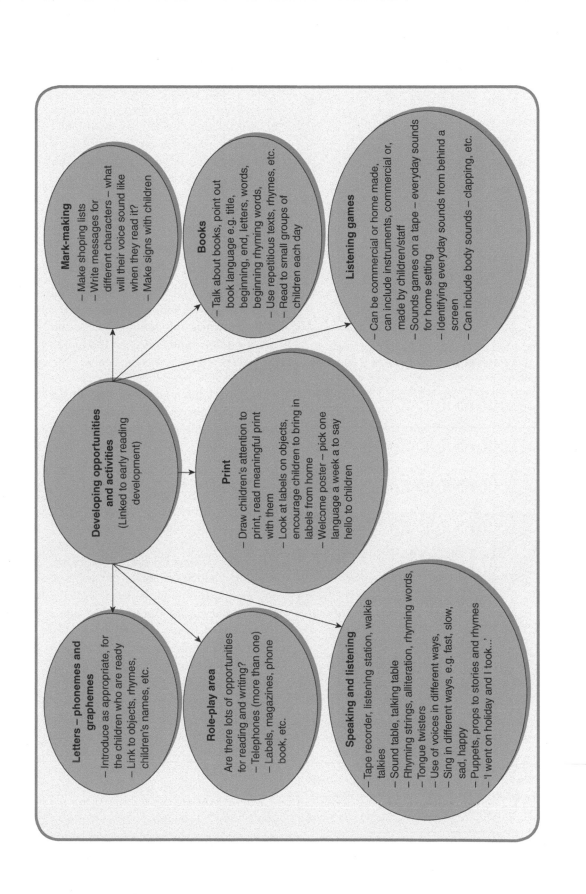

Mark-making
- Make shoping lists
- Write messages for different characters – what will their voice sound like when they read it?
- Make signs with children

Books
- Talk about books, point out book language e.g. title, beginning, end, letters, words, beginning rhyming words,
- Use repetitious texts, rhymes, etc.
- Read to small groups of children each day

Listening games
- Can be commercial or home made, can include instruments, commercial or, made by children/staff
- Sounds games on a tape – everyday sounds for home setting
- Identifying everyday sounds from behind a screen
- Can include body sounds – clapping, etc.

Developing opportunities and activities
(Linked to early reading development)

Print
- Draw children's attention to print, read meaningful print with them
- Look at labels on objects, encourage children to bring in labels from home
- Welcome poster – pick one language a week a to say hello to children

Letters – phonemes and graphemes
- Introduce as appropriate, for the children who are ready
- Link to objects, rhymes, children's names, etc.

Role-play area
- Are there lots of opportunities for reading and writing?
- Telephones (more than one)
- Labels, magazines, phone book, etc.

Speaking and listening
- Tape recorder, listening station, walkie talkies
- Sound table, talking table
- Rhyming strings, alliteration, rhyming words,
- Tongue twisters
- Use of voices in different ways,
- Sing in different ways, e.g. fast, slow, sad, happy
- Puppets, props to stories and rhymes
- 'I went on holiday and I took...'

Displays should have a clear focus and not be cluttered. This is a simple display for Elmer the elephant, containing the book and a prop. The childminder delights in offering book displays, often placed at ground level for very young children. These are based on observations of particular children's interests and are planned with these in mind

The charts (see pages 44–5) show different ways of helping children to participate in their culture, and to learn about other cultures in ways that are manageable for them. Children need all of this as part of a rich language and literature environment.

Meaningful print

Displays – less is more

It is often the case that practitioners fill every bit of wall with print or a display; and sometimes this will spill over and cover windows and doors. All this makes for a cluttered environment. It also:

- makes children edgy, with an impact on behaviour, because it is not calming;
- is impossible to see the print for all the clutter.

Favourite words – especially the child's name

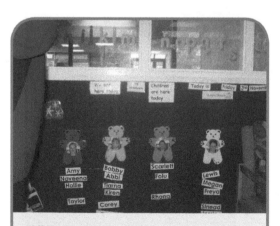

Children need meaningful print, such as their names. They are then more likely to look at this. Children enjoy picking out their name, and they will also know that it will appear under a bear in their group colour. This is how the key person groups have been organized in this pre-school

One of the things we discussed when we met for our training session was pioneering work by Sylvia Ashton Warner that took place in New Zealand in the 1950s. She noted and wrote down the favourite and emotionally important words of the children she taught. Each day she asked them to read their words, and any they could not remember were thrown away. In this way they built up a sight vocabulary (word recognition) which engaged their interest because it was made up of those words that were important to them. Sylvia Ashton Warner understood that reading words needed to engage children's feelings, interests and relationships with people they loved as well as their thoughts.

The childminder made a set of 'special words' with her children. They included words like 'plane', 'tiger', 'digger', 'train' and 'dragon' and the child's name. The name was put on the shoe-box in which their special words were kept.

Children's names are important to them as the 'first fixed string' of letters making a word

Names are part of the way children build their identity and they are of emotional importance. This is a very good example of the need that Margaret Meek (in Goouch and Lambirth, 2007) emphasizes for reading to connect with children at an emotional as well as a thoughtful level. Our names are hugely emotional. To read your name, and later to be able to write it, is an emotional experience for a young child. It is a celebration of the self. Margaret Meek has argued tirelessly that children need rich content in what they read.

A box of special words for the child. Loui loves dragons and diggers, and his childminder has collected small world props, and made labels for each. He knows it is a 'treasure box' for him because it has his photograph on the outside, and his name, which he has recognized and tried to write on the outside

Self-registration

Children can find their photograph and put it in a box to show they have arrived. They might also be encouraged to find their name and put it next to their photograph

Placemats with the words a child has chosen on them

Children enjoy choosing favourite words and seeing the practitioner write these on the placemat they use for snacks and meals. Sometimes these may be themed. A child might be invited to choose a favourite fruit, as William had done in the figure (right).

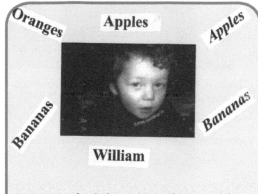

In one pre-school playgroup, cards were made out of the fruit the children liked and had chosen. The child's photograph was on the card, as were the words for the fruit together with pictures

Noticing letters and words indoors and outdoors

Children will often notice and learn words like EXIT or CLOSED, or if they live in London and journey on tube trains they might notice, written on the edge of the platform, 'Mind the Gap'.

Poetry cards

These give children small, manageable chunks of text in large print. Poetry cards are invaluable. (These are explored in a later chapter.)

Sequencing cards to support children in retelling stories and rhymes

The story is set out in a sequence of pictures which the children arrange in order. This helps children to narrate (tell) the story.

Children mark-making and writing

There should be a mark-making area with a carefully selected and presented range of paper and pencils, felt pens and crayons. It is helpful if this place is near to the workshop area, with scissors, glues, masking tapes, string, hole punchers, etc. Children often want to make cards and books, and need to have the material to do so.

The clutter issue raises itself again. Depending on the number of children using the area, it is best to have two of each coloured pencil, a few black-leaded pencils, and a few sheets of each size of

This is 'e' for eggs. The chickens on our farm laid the eggs in the photograph

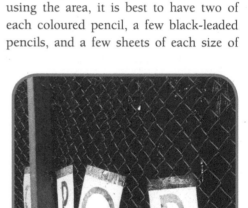

Rory found 'R' for Rory on the outdoor alphabet

Children can sort out the order of events in a story. Doing this with simple nursery rhymes makes a manageable beginning

paper and envelopes, etc. If there are too many, children will not take care of the area and clearing up time will become a nightmare. If children know where everything goes, and can see the labels on pots and baskets – saying '6 black pencils', '4 right-handed pairs of scissors', '2 left-handed pairs of scissors', '3 small envelopes', etc. – they are seeing meaningful print which will guide them to put things in the right places. It also helps those children who are ready to do so to read the captions.

Movement, dance and music

The importance of these is woven throughout the book.

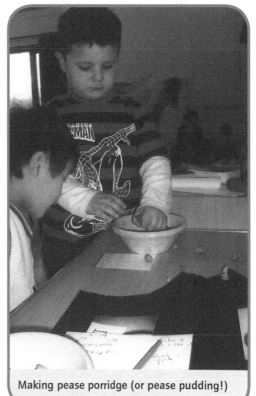

'Horsey, horsey don't you stop/Let your feet go clippety clop'. Making and finding musical and rhythmic sounds

Going to the shop is a long way. We looked at some fish

Making the wall for Humpty Dumpty in the garden

Making pease porridge (or pease pudding!)

Making gingerbread men after hearing the story

Powerful first-hand experiences which support children's understanding of rhymes

Gingerbread Man

Making gingerbread biscuits helps children to make more sense of the story of the gingerbread man.

Making a wall

It is a good experience to use three-dimensional props when acting out nursery rhymes. Boys especially are more likely to become involved (DCSF, 2007). In the photograph on the previous page children are making a wall in the garden and there is a good balance of boys and girls choosing to take part.

Making an organic garden

Children became enthusiastic gardeners in one pre-school playgroup. They linked this with the rhyme, 'Mary, Mary Quite Contrary'.

If children are looking at spiders and other mini-beasts, it makes sense to have non-fiction, information books on the subject on a small table display in the garden, together with the magnifier pots. Having cards with the names of spiders, ants, woodlice, and so on printed on them together with a suitable picture or photograph is also helpful

Places where people tend to chat and make conversations

Sitting round the fire, cooking dampers, having conversations, exchanging ideas, singing songs. This is a good place to sit and think as well

OPENING UP THE WORLD OF COMMUNICATION, LANGUAGE AND LITERACY IN AN ENABLING ENVIRONMENT

Observing the uniqueness of each child's learning journey from birth to seven years enables us to:

- build on that child's individual interests and needs
- work in partnership with parents and carers, as a team
- explore and track that child's progress
- inform our planning, both for individual children and for the group as a whole
- work with other practitioners who are important to the child
- see that child as a unique individual
- see how interconnected the different areas of development and learning are.

In this chapter we have focussed on how and what adults need to offer in order to create enabling environments for rich communication, language and literacy.

KEY TERMS

These terms are used in this chapter and throughout the book.

Narrative observation – this kind of observation helps to assess where the child is in learning about communication, language and literacy. It is given a central place in official documents which are legally enshrined. It involves a description of what a child is doing, saying and communicating, followed by analysis, and this informs planning for the child

(Continued)

(Continued)

Connected language – this is about the way that words join together, with prepositions, clauses and phrases and the use of tenses to give a few examples

Eye movements – these fixate on a word, or scan ahead and back (saccades). More is covered on these later on, but it is important to become familiar with the term early on

Predicting – one of the most important aspects of reading is the ability to predict what is coming next. Fluent readers can do this. Emergent readers come in two types (Meek, 2007): some cling to sounding-out words correctly, and tend to lose the sense and the flow; others need to flow and in order to do that will insert inaccurate readings, but they usually self correct and will go back to correct this because they are keen to keep the meaning of the text

Approximate reading – children begin to realize that what they say can be written down, so they will delight in knowing the words of a rhyme or story and then pointing. They move their finger along the line of the text, and gradually they realize that each word can be pointed to on the page

Fixed string – children begin to learn that letters can be strung together to make a word. Their name is often the first fixed string they engage with, and this is emotionally satisfying for them

Reading

Bruce, T., Meggitt, C. and Grenier, J. (2010) *Childcare and Education* (5th edn). London: Hodder. Read the sections on the development of communication, language and literacy, and the sections on observation.

Further Reading

Meek, M., Warlow, A. and Barton, G. (1977) *The Cool Web: The Patterns of Children's Reading*. London, Sydney, Toronto: Bodley Head. This is a classic that will help remind you that it is just as important to focus on what children are going to read, and how they feel about stories and songs and rhymes they are introduced to, as well as all the other aspects of the journey into literacy, which need to be embedded in communication, language, feelings, ideas, thoughts, relationships, the physical body, and culture.

Chapter 3

Parent/Baby Songs

In this chapter we show how:

- the brain develops, including emotion and feeling;
- we can help babies and very young children to communicate;
- we can encourage babies and young children to participate in social and cultural life.

The development of the brain

People often mistakenly believe that brain development is only about the physical development of a child but this is only part of the story. Brain development is also largely about the social and emotional development of children, as well as an increasing ability to think and have ideas (Goddard-Blythe, 2004; Trevarthen, 2004; Blakemore and Frith, 2005).

We need to explore the multi-sensory world of the child as a crucial aspect of learning. We are constantly looking at the importance of sound, sight, feel and touch, smells and tastes and, very important, the movement and feedback from movements made. Penny Greenland (2010) emphasizes the importance of movement as the 'felt sense of life'. Elizabeth Harrison (1895), writing about Friedrich Froebel's early kindergartens, understood the child's need for movement by stating 'the effect of the body upon the mind is not generally appreciated'.

We are beginning to gain a deeper knowledge of the link between the body and the brain, through the neurosciences and also through cognitive psychology.

An integral part of life from the moment of conception until death, and a child's experience of movement plays a pivotal part in shaping his/her personality, his/her feelings and his achievements. Learning is not just about reading, writing and maths. These are higher abilities that are built upon the integrity of the relationship between brain and body. (Goddard-Blythe, 2004: 5)

The first few months – looking, listening and moving

Listening – the beginnings of phonological awareness

Even in their first month, babies react to the sounds around them – loud sounds, particular music, the voices of their parents and close family. This will be important later on when they learn to read and write. Literacy is rooted in being aware of sounds and also in being able to discriminate between similar sounds, where they come from and how they are made, with increasing awareness. Phonological awareness 'refers to the ability to hear sounds' (Mallett, 2005: 243).

Looking – the sound of voices comes out of mouths

In their first month, babies will stare at human faces and be fascinated by them. A newborn baby 'can be alert to the face of a sympathetic caregiver speaking, drawing comfort from the expression of affection carried by the eyes and the loving voice' (Trevarthen, 2004: 5).

This is an important part of being fed, and babies who are bottle-fed can lose out on this experience unless they are held close like a breastfed baby. Babies (Murray and Andrews, 2000: 8–9) will look intently at facial expressions, and a person's mouth as it moves while talking to them. They will stick out their tongue if someone does that to them (though you have to wait patiently for them to imitate this). They will also move in response to someone if they say 'hallo' in an excited way, or smile at them – so much so that neuroscientist Colwyn Trevarthen says it is as if a baby is dancing with another person, moving together and responding to one another's faces. This subtle kind of imitation is an essential aspect of the journey that a child take into literacy.

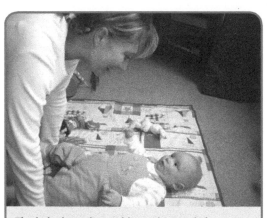

The baby is gazing at his mother, and she returns the gaze and talks to him. This is important in developing communication and language. The tone of voice, rhythm, pauses, turn-taking and other aspects are all important parts of this. Babies will track people they love as they move about

Babies will also fix on faces and will track them and other objects as they move. Later on fixating and tracking will become important in the development of reading and writing. Eye movements are studied by researchers (Rayner et al., (2007) who are interested in how this is used when someone is reading. We know that gazing and tracking are important for babies. Work on later fixating and scanning (saccades) suggests that children who have developed rich experiences that help their thinking to develop will be able to fixate on a word for less time, which means they can read ahead and be more fluent. Beginner readers do this if words are familiar through experience of life beyond the text.

Movement – feedback

We also see babies moving their head in order to follow adult movements, or to track where a brother or sister moves across the room.

For the purposes of this chapter, one of the most exciting aspects of the baby's development in the first month is the way they hold their hands tightly closed, and often tuck their thumbs in under their fingers (Bruce, Meggitt and Grenier, 2010: 42–3).

They open their hands in order to grasp someone's finger. One of Tina's most wonderful memories is, when she was three years and six months old, seeing her baby brother a few hours after his birth, and putting her little finger next to his closed hand. He opened it and grasped her finger. From that moment on they bonded and she has loved him deeply ever since.

We begin to see babies watching their hands and playing with their fingers. They might hold something like a rattle for a short time before dropping it. They are beginning to sort out that people make sounds as do objects.

In the next few months, babies will often play with their toes and feet when they are lying on their backs. This is because the spine is developing its strength and they can reach further. It is also helping the gaze to fixate further away from the hands towards the feet. Changing the focus is important in the development of eye movements, and this becomes important later on when children learn to read.

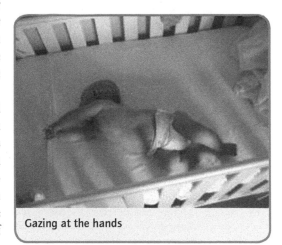

Gazing at the hands

The brain is part of the central nervous system. The other parts of the nervous system are the spinal cord and the peripheral system (which includes the sensory nerves for input and motor nerves for acting out what the brain says). The central nervous system has a genetically programmed sequence of development. Put simply, it develops from 'tail to head'. The top of the head, the cerebral cortex region of the brain, develops last. (Meade, 2003: 6)

Parents and carers interacting with very young children through movement and non-verbal communication in dance-like ways

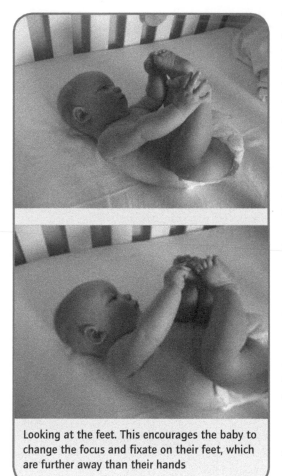

Looking at the feet. This encourages the baby to change the focus and fixate on their feet, which are further away than their hands

The work of Colwyn Trevarthen (2004: 3) at Edinburgh University has, across the years, shown that babies in their first three months are able to take part in what he calls 'proto-conversations'. It is as if babies are 'born to find someone who communicates interest and affection'.

Babies are biologically driven to make their families engage with their smiles, coo vocalizations, and make hand gestures, and are able to tell us when they want to socialize through a gaze approach, or when they need a rest from 'chatting' through using gaze avoidance.

By the time they can sit, Trevarthen (2004: 2) has found that babies can 'negotiate interests, intentions and feelings' with two other babies at a similar point in their development and learning, without the help of adults. They use imitation as a way of setting up communication. If one baby picks up an object from the treasure basket, others do the same, and often take these from each other.

Before this, newborn babies 'imitate simple expressions of face, hands or voice, and expect to get a response from the person they are attending to' (Trevarthen, 2004: 3).

Sympathy neurons in the brain

It has become clear that the cells in which 'mirroring' effects have been recorded are part of widely distributed systems through the brain, that both move and feel with another subject. It might be better to call these neural mechanisms of *sympathy*, which is the Greek word meaning 'moving and feeling with'. (Trevarthen, 2004: 6)

One of the themes throughout this book is the way that children understand things before they can perform. They can hear the sound 'j' before they can articulate it. Understanding precedes competence. Competence precedes performance. This is so for a baby's ability to understand the mechanics of having a 'conversation' before words are possible.

It is therefore very important for babies and young children to spend time with adults who can help them to develop understanding as they see, hear and move.

The baby, aged, fifteen months, sits on his mother's knee inside the Oogly Boogly dome. This is a neutral space and soft music is playing, so that it is not silent. The baby feels secure and bangs his foot on the padded floor. It makes a thudding sound.

The actor, sitting opposite the baby, bangs his foot in the same way, mirroring the baby's action. The baby looks at the actor for a moment, and then lifts his foot and pulls his sock off.

The actor lifts his foot and pulls his sock off. The baby realises the actor is copying him and that whatever he does, the actor will do it. The baby also realises that he is the one in control of the game. (Observation, Spratt, 2006)

The whole focus of the theatre company's 'Oogly Boogly' experience is based on observation. The actors and dancers taking part in the play have spent a long time focussing on how to observe the sounds, postures, facial expressions, eye-pointing, gaze, intonation, tone, rhythm and movement of the babies they work with. The work of the theatre company shows how non-verbal communication between actor and child, sitting safely on their parent's knee to begin with, provides a signal for the adult. The child is on the edge or cusp of spoken language. The 'Oogly Boogly' experience is therefore only for babies typically aged from 12 to 18 months (or children at a similar point of development) as they are developing:

- a sense of physical self-embodiment
- a sense of themselves as a thinker (meta-cognition)
- a sense of their feelings and their management of them (emotional literacy)
- on the cusp of language.

Judy Dunne (1988) also comments on the way babies delight in their parents and family, echoing back what they say and how they move.

Damasio (2004) suggests a 'nesting principle' where the baby is laying down the foundations for communication and later reading and writing.

This links with the work of Roberto Frabetti, who creates theatre for very young children. He proposes that:

Listening is complex – it means paying attention to what is not said, to the hidden, to the evoked ... the children's eyes and silences go hand in hand and sometimes they open doors to hidden worlds. Most of the time we are not able to see them, and then we lose a good chance to be astonished. (2005: 64)

The silences and pauses of very young children as we interact with them are important ways by which they build up their understanding and ability to communicate. Children's pauses are 'Long pauses that make you consider time from a different point of view' (Frabetti, 2005: 70).

Babies have a fine sense of timing and rhythm in conversations

We can find, in the first three months:

- syllabic beat
- phrasing

- sympathetic co-ordination of movements, looking and sounds between baby and familiar, loved adult
- call and response
- emphasis and intonation.

The work of Gunilla Preisler at Stockholm University shows that blind babies will take part in these proto-conversations too. In this extract a mother and her blind five-month-old daughter share a song:

> Their delicate and subtle duetting is made even more instructive by the fact that this infant was born totally and permanently blind. She has never seen her hands or the hands of any other person. And yet it appears she can accompany portions of the song her mother sings with expressive hand gestures that display intelligent precision and even some anticipation of melody. Over the past months the baby girl has become very familiar with these compositions by Alice Tegnar, whose children's songs are much loved throughout Scandinavia. (Trevarthen, 1999–2000: 186)

Hands and language go together. We naturally use our hands as we speak. Trevarthen suggests that hand movements add emotive meaning to what we say. The two systems, hand gestures and speaking, develop in an integrated way. Sitting on our hands while we speak makes it almost impossible to say what we want to say!

As parents, the Papouseks found their baby daughter, at four months, was using their parental tones and rhythms: 'A diary of their daughter documented the infant's enjoyment of nursery songs, and her private practice of acquired musical forms' (Trevarthen, 2004: 9).

Daniel Stern also notes that the way the parent or carer picks up the baby's expressions is very significant. For example, this has far-reaching implications for children in group care and the importance of babies in group care having a key person cannot be overemphasized. Note that this is a central part of the *Early Years Foundation Stage*.

Parent/baby songs

Once again, Froebel (1782–1852) stands out as a pioneer educator who realized the importance of singing to babies and involving them in movement play. He did this through his 'Mother Songs', thus raising the status of motherhood at a time when babies were farmed out to be cared for by wet nurses, and often had little or no contact with their parents. The recent research we have touched on demonstrates the importance of these early forms of introduction to music and dance through movement, looking at each other and listening. Imitation is key to this. Trevarthen and colleagues have collected what they call 'Baby Songs' in many languages. These resonate with Froebel's 'Mother Songs'.

Trevarthen and colleagues have also found that parent/baby songs in English have these characteristics:

- they are typically four stanzas long with four simple phrases
- there is often a rhyming pattern at the end of the second and fourth lines.

Cheerful parent/baby songs

These show the following aspects:

- the rhythm is often a dancing rhythm
- the base pulse is *andante*, which means it is at walking pace
- there are variations in rhythm to give excitement in the last two lines
- there are simple shifts of pitch
- it is easy for babies (who are often only four months old) to predict the timing and rhyming features of the song.

For example, a baby might sing on top of the mother's singing: in the following it would be exactly on top of the word 'bear'.

> Round and round the garden
> Like a teddy bear
> One step, two step
> Tickly under there

Lullabies to soothe

These show the following characteristics:

- the rhythm is often slower than the walking pace of *andante*. It is *adagio* and soothing, with a gentle rocking rhythm
- it is soothing in pitch, without any moments of excitement.

For example, the song might be

> Bye Baby Bunting
> Daddy's gone a-hunting
> Gone to fetch a rabbit skin
> To wrap a Baby Bunting in.

Babies become interested in objects as well as people

At around three months old a baby's hands begin to open out from the tight little fists they have been. They start to grasp and release objects, so we often put rattles into their hands. But this interest in objects

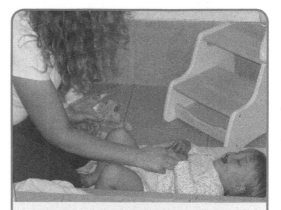

'Round and round the garden/Like a teddy bear/One step, two step/Tickly under there/' This song has all the features outlined above. There is a dancing rhythm, and the rhyme goes at a walking pace, from low to high. The last lines are hugely exciting with the lead up to the tickling, and there is a simple shift of pitch. The song is very accessible for the babies

comes long after their engagement with people, as we have explored so far in this chapter: 'Objects are now discovered at an accelerating pace, by the combined application of hands, eyes, ears and mouth to pick up useful information' (Trevarthen, 2004: 14).

From the beginning, we hang a mobile above the cradle for the baby to look at. Penny Greenland (2010) points out that, as children develop and need to try out stretching, they need mobiles they can reach for, and objects they can hold with an arm extended. It is the same with the toes. We often see babies stretching out a leg to kick a toy in their cradle. They will be on their back, but the satisfaction registers on their face as the foot makes contact and they feel the connection. As they do this stretching, babies are changing the focus of their eyes from near to far, which will be important in later reading.

Hayden, because he is mobile, can select the objects he wants. He pushes away a second soft ball and keeps the other one. The soft ball is a favourite, and this is typical of crawling babies. He knows he can make the ball roll away from him, and he likes to watch this. It is exercising, quite naturally, his developing ability to track a moving object along a trajectory. Later he will need his tracking ability to follow a line of print in a text.

Parents/key persons beginning movement play

Trevarthen and colleagues show that after the first three months parents tend to engage their babies in movement play with stronger forces and rhythms, sharing the drama, excitement and laughter: 'Soon play routines are discovered that facilitate lively and enthusiastic participation and make the baby laugh when half-expected surprises occur, or when the baby knows they are coming' (Trevarthen, 2004: 14). Later this will turn into the rough and tumble play which Penny Greenland (2006) emphasizes at the toddler stage of development, when children are moving on to walking, talking and pretending.

Before children are mobile, the baby songs have an important place. The adult tickles the child, and initiates movement accompanied by a song. In this chapter, we have seen this in the rhythm of 'Round and Round the Garden Like a Teddy Bear'. This means that looking, listening and moving are being co-ordinated in the service of communication and language development. This develops into finger rhymes. The importance of the hand therefore continues with the refinement of the use of fingers.

The adult engages the baby in songs

This little piggy went to market

This little piggy stayed at home
This little piggy ate roast beef
This little piggy had none
This little piggy went
Wee wee wee
All the way home.

Sharing jokes and laughter

These are important both with baby songs and tickling games. Bateson (1995) showed that in addition to jokes and laughter, grammatical rules, poetic and dramatic forms with narrative plots as well as rules of music and dance nest in baby songs. During all this fun and laughter babies are communicating about communicating, which is called 'meta-communication'.

Hands as objects

In an earlier section in this chapter, we looked at the importance of objects for babies. However we need to be careful here.

> In a modern home there are electronic toys that are programmed to play tunes or carry out spontaneous simulations of human or animal action. Such 'robots' are exciting, indeed – but we have to wonder if they threaten to eliminate interaction such as a baby can only have with a live mind in a live body. (Trevarthen, 2004: 15–16)

Froebel's understanding of the importance of 'Mother Songs', which Trevarthen and colleagues write about as 'Baby Songs', makes a major contribution to the developing learning of babies about communication and language, in which later literacy nests.

Pat-a-cake, pat-a-cake

Baker's man
Bake me a cake
As fast as you can
Pat it and prick it
And mark it with 'B'
Put it in the oven for baby and me
Baby and me, baby and me
Put it in the oven
For baby and me.

IN SUMMARY

The parent or key person encourages the use of the hands in these songs. This paves the way for finger rhymes, which are explored in the next chapter, and shows:

- the importance of the baby's relationship with warm, affectionate parents, siblings and key people
- how we can be helpful to children in developing communication and language from the moment a baby is born, because that baby has a need to learn by picking up ideas from a community of people they love

(Continued)

(Continued)

- how babies use imitation and mirroring to co-ordinate the integrated strands of movements, looking and listening
- how early we see babies showing their intention to communicate with us, and an ability to engage in proto-conversations, because this is how they begin to learn about what other people know and do
- how music and dance are there from the beginning, and how they support the essentials of later literacy, such as rhythm, rhyme, intonation and alliteration.

Key Terms

Adagio – slower than walking pace

Andante – at walking pace

Iambic beat – a dancing beat

Neurosciences – the scientific study of the brain and nervous system, which has traditionally been seen as a branch of biology

Reading

Greenland, P. (2010) 'Physical development', in T. Bruce (ed.), *Early Childhood: A Guide for Students* (2nd edn). London: SAGE.

Further Reading

Goddard-Blythe, S. (2004) *The Well-Balanced Child – Movement and Early Learning.* Stroud: Hawthorn Press.

Chapter 4

Finger Rhymes

In this chapter we show how:

- the brain co-ordinates the hands, eyes and ears;
- practitioners and carers can use finger rhymes to support this developmental process.

The relationship between finger rhymes and action songs – on the spot and moving around

It might come as something of a surprise to find that this chapter (about songs using finger and hand movements) comes before the next two chapters (mark-making, writing and action songs, moving around). This is because it is often still taught that fine motor movements develop later than gross motor movements. They do – but one helps the other along. So it is not right to think of these in a totally hierarchical and linear way. With the development of knowledge in the neurosciences and brain studies we now know that the two go along together, and that the body supports the hand and the head. The hand (including the fingers), eyes, sound and mouth, are of central importance, established in the first few months and becoming increasingly co-ordinated as babies reach out to grasp objects. By crawling (which opens out the hands as the child places them on the ground) and pointing (in the first year) the hands become further developed. Contact with the ground sends important messages to the brain, helping the child to locate themselves in relation to the ground (proprioception) which is vital for developing movement and mobility in general. In this book we have outlined a carefully thought through approach that supports and extends these natural hand/finger movements. On-the-spot action songs can go alongside finger rhymes, but these emerge from the development of the hand/eye/ear co-ordinations in the first year of life. These on-the-spot action songs include changes of focus from distant to near, greater tracking of arm movements, and more complicated words and actions to carry out. Because locomotion action songs require significantly more co-ordination, as they include moving the legs at the same time as doing the actions and singing, they come later developmentally. That is why that chapter has been placed later in the book.

> It is important to work with and not against nature. Parents and key people are of central importance.
> By the time a baby is sitting, a great deal has been going on with the baby's developing vision, proprioception (feeling where their body is located with reference to the floor) and balance (the midline) so that they operate together. The hands continue to play an important part in the developing learning.
> The baby's hearing is developing fast, and the rhythms, and sounds the baby makes are resonant with the language(s) the baby hears and will speak. The babble changes at about 6 weeks of age, so that the baby begins to lose sounds that are not around him or her, keeping those of the language(s) heard. (Trevarthen, 2004)

Sitting – looking at fingers and thumbs

Tiny babies knead and grip as they feed at the breast, using a palmar grip. It is more difficult to knead a bottle. The movement encourages sucking, and the milk to flow from the mother. This link between mouth and hand is called the Babkin response (Goddard-Blythe, 2004). Being able to grip is important. But so is learning how to let go of objects at will. When sitting babies drop toys over the edge of their highchair, that is exactly what is happening! This will be important for the child's pencil control later on.

This palmar grasp is followed by the pincer grasp. A baby will use their index finger and thumb in opposition to transfer a toy from one hand to the other, and to put objects in their mouths. Sally Goddard-Blythe (2004: 52) stresses the importance of the development of such co-ordinations between hand and mouth. She says these co-ordinations are 'cortical maps' for the brain. Some babies seem to blink as they suck, especially premature babies. There is a connection here between what the baby sees, sucking the hand that brings an object to the mouth, and speech articulation.

The baby who is able to sit unaided will experiment with reaching for objects in front of them, behind them, and on the opposite side to the hand with which they reach. There is plenty of toppling over as they work out how to balance around their midline. But this does not put the baby off. Penny

Greenland (2010: 190), who is Director of the Developmental Movement Centre, says that – fortunately – babies are biologically driven to 'seek out, and create, the experiences they need'. She goes on to say, 'It is active involvement and exploration through movement play that enables a child to become a more mature, efficient organiser of sensory information – providing the foundations for all future learning.'

Crawling – balancing and travelling at the same time

Children need to spend plenty of time on the floor. Penny Greenland (2010) suggests that:

- being on their back or tummy helps children to sense their bodies as they kick their feet and move their hands
- being able to sit is important because you don't topple over, and can manage to stay that way when you reach around you for objects
- being able to crawl is important for future learning because it 'supports a strong sense of the centre of the body whilst in motion' (Greenland, 2010), and it is the first time that children will experience balancing and travelling at the same time
- it is the first time that children can look from side to side without moving their head from side to side as they travel along, and this will be important later when learning to read.

Sitting and crawling are part of the journey from being curled up in the womb – like a letter 'C' says Penny Greenland (2006), becoming the 'S' shape of the spine as we stand up.

As children develop, some doors shut as others open in the brain. Sarah-Jayne Blakemore and Uta Frith (2005: 31) explain, 'New learning means opening and setting neural connections for important events and closing others that are no longer important and would only be distracting and confusing.'

Babies need to spend time sitting on the floor and crawling so that the closing down of some movements can occur naturally,

Looking ahead and from side to side without moving the head while travelling along lays the foundations for the later tracking that eye movements will undertake when reading. Children who are not well co-ordinated are likely to encounter difficulties in learning to read and write. Clumsy children find later pencil control difficult, and also the fine focus on words when tracking print on a page. They lose confidence easily because of this. Experiences throughout early childhood and beyond which develop movement are crucial in learning to read and write later on and in the process open the way for others. If they do not fade, the child could later experience difficulty in sitting still at a table or on a chair.

Building on natural development

During our work together, Jenny led the group in a piece of professional development work that emphasized finger rhymes were more important than we had known previously. For this reason we are devoting a whole chapter to this aspect of learning.

Babies, sitters, crawlers and wobbly walkers are learning the things which will be important to them later on. Sally Goddard-Blythe (2004: 65) says, 'reflex movements in nerve cells lie at the root of every act of higher will: the highest acts of will merely have deliberation, choice, and inhibition added to these foundation reflexes'. Neuroscientist Antonio Damasio says the same thing in a different way. He says a child's development

> consists of having parts of simpler reactions incorporated as components of more elaborate ones, a nesting principle of the simple within the complex ... Each of the different regulatory reactions is not a radically different process, built from scratch for a specific purpose. Rather, each reaction consists of tinkered rearrangements of bits and parts of the simpler processes below. They are all aimed at the same overall goal – survival with well-being – but each of the tinkered rearrangements is secondarily aimed at a new problem whose solution is necessary for the overall goal to be achieved. (Damasio, 2004: 37–8)

Put simply, this means:

- babies and toddlers who get appropriate support there and then are also being helped in their future learning
- we need to know the key aspects of a child's development in communication, relationships, language, play and movement
- we also need to know what is involved in the subject knowledge of reading and writing (literacy), literature and information.

The best image for capturing this is that of a tree: 'a tall messy tree with progressively higher and more elaborate branches coming off the main trunks and thus maintaining a two-way communication with the roots. The history of evolution is written all over that tree' (Damasio, 2004: 38).

Penny Greenland and Sally Goddard-Blythe both point out that most children pass through these sequences of development with ease, naturally playing and becoming walkers with all the important developmental building blocks in place. It is important to emphasize that we need to create rich learning environments with an atmosphere of warm affection, encouraging children to develop and learn, as reflected in the official documents of the four countries of the UK, and are also central in Te Whāriki in New Zealand, and in the approach of Reggio Emilia in Northern Italy. These have remained every time the official documents have been changed in these different countries.

Playing at being a dog, and crawling as part of that, or making a den under a table, all contributes to the ability to use hands and fingers to the full. When a child crawls, two important things happen to the hand:

- the hand is spread out
- leaning on the floor puts pressure on the palm of the hand, which the child then feels – feedback which helps to locate the body so that it is, quite literally, well grounded.

Finger songs and rhymes link sound, sight and movement

Finger rhymes build on natural development helping to co-ordinate hand and mouth movements, by looking and remembering, by the rhythm, and matching sight with sound. They extend the learning we covered in the last chapter. All of these are important for developing the essentials of literacy and a love of literature, and in seeking knowledge and information.

The ability to match sounds and sights takes years to develop, but it is very important in learning how to read and write. Finger rhymes help the process along in ways that are for toddlers and young children. They form an important early part of the journey that a child takes into literacy.

When babies hear a sound, they often freeze and listen carefully. They are waiting to find out if it brings comfort or danger. When they hear an unfamiliar sound they also open their eyes wide in a startled response and then look from place to place to try and see the source of the sound. They fix their eyes on it.

This helps toddlers and young children to co-ordinate sound, sight and movement which in turn helps children towards their future reading and writing.

Singing at the same time as doing the finger movements, each in co-ordination with the other, is a huge challenge for young children. The concentration is deep. The co-ordination of the words and sounds with getting the fingers into position, together with the need to look at the fingers to guide and check this process, are fundamentally important as they mean the brain is encouraged to bring together hand/eye/hand movements. This will be used when learning to read and write

The three-year-old boy said to his key person, 'I can do my ruby ring now.' He held up his finger to show her and started to sing, with his hands behind his back, 'Ruby ring, ruby ring, where are you?'. He then brought his hands out in front, raised his fourth fingers and sang, 'Here I am, here I am, how do you do?' He was linking the appropriate finger with the movement and the words of the song.

How it looks

Another child, also three years old, often likes to wear his Spiderman outfit to the early childhood setting. He too has learnt the Tommy Thumb finger rhyme. One day he sang his key person a song he had created himself, based on this. He put his hand behind his back, and sang, 'Spiderman, Spiderman, where are you?' He brought his hands out in front of him and put his fingers into a shape where he clenched each hand, but put his second and third finger out. He thrust the hand forward in time to the rhythm and sang, 'Here I am, here I am, how do you do?'

This is a variation on a theme, which is a strategy by which creativity often presents itself (Bruce, 2004a: 97).

Trying to 'do my ruby ring.' It is a great challenge for a young child to achieve the different finger movements and positions for the song, 'Tommy Thumb, Tommy Thumb, Where Are You?' He is, quite rightly, thrilled with his achievement of the most difficult finer placement in this much loved finger rhyme

Sorting out sounds – phonological awareness

When we sing, we extend the vowel sounds, and this helps the phonological awareness which will be crucial in learning to read later on. It helps children to hear the specific sounds of the language, and because singing accentuates vowels, it aids the later reading of words. The work of Goswami and colleagues (in Goouch and Lambirth, 2007) shows that the English language is very inconsistent and so this makes it more difficult to read and write than if a child was learning to read and write in Italian, for example. Eventually the child will be able to distinguish the differences between the sounds of the language, but singing and moving to finger rhymes helps the brain to engage with this process in ways that are appropriate to the child's development. Finger rhymes help children towards becoming aware of syllables, rhyming chunks, and later phonemic awareness in enjoyable and unpressured ways.

Tooooooooooommy Thuuuuuuumb, Tooooooooommy Thuuuuuuumb
Wheeeeeeere aaaaaaare yoooooooou?
Heeeeeeere I am, Heeeeeere I am,
Hooooooow do you dooooooo?

Tomatis (in Goddard-Blythe, 2004) says that using the voice in singing helps children (including children with hearing impairments) to develop their listening skills. Children need to be able to distinguish between the different sounds of a language. Adam Ockelford (1996) has developed songs about everyday situations, such as greetings, partings and meals, to help children with visual and complex needs communicate. Singing 'It's dinner time' often brings a response, when simply saying it does not. In Chapter 3 on parent/baby songs the example was given of a mother singing to her blind baby, and the baby participating and moving in response. It is important to note that singing and moving while doing so is often an important way of working with children with special educational needs and disabilities.

Finger rhymes help children to develop the rhythm of language-syllables

Hearing words in a song helps children to develop an understanding of rhythms and syllabification, which is crucial in later reading. Rhythm is a sequence of movements in time.

Toh mmee Thumb.

It is easy to sense that 'Tommy' has two syllables and 'Thumb' only has one. This does not have to be discussed with a young child, they feel it through the rhythm of the finger rhyme.

Finger rhymes give children memory aids which help language to develop

Finger rhymes help children to develop their memory, which is important in learning a sight vocabulary in later reading. The senses inform the body, and in addition finger rhymes introduce the symbolic aspects of developing learning. Not all children will be able to learn finger rhymes. Some children with disabilities will enjoy the music, and perhaps join in with the singing and music making, but will be constrained physically.

Marian Whitehead (2010) reminds us that it is easier remembering a rhyme than remembering the words in ordinary language.

Finger rhymes help the relationship between the young child and the parent, older sibling or key person, as well as developing muscles

The relationships children have with people they spend time with are of fundamental importance.

Children do not develop good language unless they are spoken to in an atmosphere of warmth and affection. Communication is about looking at each other as well as engaging with each other. Language development is fostered in the use of finger rhymes, because children are looking at the adult in order to imitate the finger movements and also to sing them once they get these movements under control. Singing and moving together is a time-honoured way of enjoying being together. It encourages an integration of movement, sound and vision in the brain.

Children love the challenge of trying to place their fingers correctly in the finger rhymes. Because they are actively moving as they do this, they have a multi-sensory experience which will help them to learn about the shape of letters and how to make them later on. This gives them direct feedback through their own body in a way that other experiences do not. This is why it is so powerful.

Finger rhymes help children to track detail, which is important when reading print later on

Children see the fingers changing from one shape to another. Children work out that they can vary the shapes and make their own – for example, we saw earlier the child who changed the one finger of the 'Tommy Thumb' rhyme into the two-fingered shape in his own composition of the 'Spiderman' song.

Enjoying the challenge. It is important that children experience feeling part of a group that is supportive and wanting everyone to succeed. In this relaxed atmosphere the children focus and engage with the finger rhyme for some time. They know they will be helped and supported to succeed, and that it is worthwhile for them to persist and put energy into their efforts. They develop staying power, and this is linked to developing good concentration. Being engaged in learning is very different from an adult setting a task and requiring a child to perform it. Children who want to become involved of their own free will know they can get help when this is needed. This is a great confidence booster

Marie Clay (1982) reminds us that young children (about six years of age typically) will scan around words on a page, rather than fixing on one word. It is important in reading to track and then converge the gaze and fix it on the word to be read. Having a fine focus on the finger and tracking it to then fix it into a shape helps this process along. However it is important here that the child and not the adult does the pointing. Since the 1980s a body of research has been growing in relation to eye movements during the reading process. This research, gathered together by Rayner, Ashby, Pollatsek and Reichle (2004), is increasingly suggesting that children will naturally fixate on the beginning or end of a word, rather than the middle. Doing this seems to be helpful for them in identifying what a word says. Children quite naturally seek out what a word begins with and grasp the rhyming end of rhymes much more easily than they will read the middle of the word. There is pressure currently to introduce synthetic phonics. This emphasizes reading through all the word, and does not allow for the natural and helpful eye movements which are less focussed on the middle. Reading makes more sense if the beginnings and ends of words can be identified. The middle can then be added. We can see this clearly in the way children develop their writing and spelling, which is the subject of the next chapter. Children write as they hear to start with, and this is very healthy in the journey into literacy. Gentry (1982), in Goouch and Lambirth (2007) demonstrates the stages of pretend writing, followed by phonetic spellings, often leaving out the vowel, and then later we can see their efforts to represent every sound in a word. Here are two examples showing this progression:

> A birthday card from four year old Hannah to her mother says, 'LV HANNAH' (Love Hannah).
> By the age of seven years Tom is writing a story, 'wans there was a swalow. He lict tofli high and swoop. Thea d'.
> (Once there was a swallow. He liked to fly high and swoop. The end.)

Finger rhymes are important for children with learning difficulties and disabilities

A child with a **learning difficulty** will need plenty of time to learn a finger rhyme, but with repetition this can be achieved. Children should not be rushed through their learning. It is important to give plenty of repetition. A child with Down's Syndrome managed to sing and use the movements for 'Two Little Birds Sitting on a Wall' after eight repetitions, and was delighted with the result. The song also needs to be sung regularly.

A child with a **visual impairment** can be taught the actions, and will often readily learn the words and tune. It is of great benefit to children if they can develop a strong sense of their own body and how it moves and feels. It is what Penny Greenland (2006) calls the 'felt sense of living'.

A child with a **hearing impairment** greatly appreciates the actions with the fingers. It helps them with a sense of rhythm, pattern and sequence which will later help them to read. It also helps children to become aware of syllabification in particular, which will help them when they later learn to read and write. Children with hearing difficulties find reading a challenge because it is so hard to co-ordinate sounds and the look of the print. Mapping sounds onto letters, and establishing the phoneme/grapheme links is not easy when much of the sound is missing. Anything that gives additional clues (often called redundancy cues) is helpful. Getting at the same information using several ways to do this assists greatly.

Introducing finger rhymes to children

Jenny Spratt explored finger rhymes as part of her studies (the Froebel Diploma, accredited by Roehampton University for the National Froebel Foundation). She became aware of the 'Mother Songs' and finger rhymes devised in the mid-nineteenth century by Friedrich Froebel. (More detail is given on the educational pioneer work of Froebel in the Introduction to this book.) Blakemore and Frith point out (2005: 128) 'research suggests that the brain assigns a quantity of synapses to the processing of the fingers in accordance with how much the fingers are used'.

What Jenny found out about finger rhymes seemed so important that we have given this a much greater emphasis. As a result we realized we had neglected them, either by lumping them together with action songs and not making a distinction between finger rhymes and action songs, or by encouraging the use of finger puppets and hand puppets as props for songs and stories. We also realized that we were not alone in doing this, and that knowledge built up by Froebel had become buried and lost.

An important Froebelian principle is to introduce the whole before isolating the parts of a finger rhyme. Jenny therefore suggested that it might be helpful to introduce the finger rhymes to children in three stages.

Stage 1

Introduce rhymes that just use the hand so that children get used to the concept of unity (Froebel) within the whole. The rhymes should involve the whole hand and all 10 fingers, opening and shutting. ('Open, shut them …')

Stage 2

Introduce rhymes that use the fingers to represent parts of the body, again supporting the child's concept of unity (Froebel). The fingers are part of the hand, which is part of the body. Different fingers are isolated during the finger rhyme. ('Tommy Thumb …')

Stage 3

Introduce rhymes that use the fingers to represent objects from nature, community, food, and so on. ('Two little dicky birds …')

Finger dexterity as emergent 'writing'

Finger rhymes enhance a child's possibility to 'write' for themselves, improving the **dexterity of their fingers** and hand control, whereas a poetry card aids their ability to recognize printed words. **Opening up** and **extending the palm** of the hand is important in this. Since many children are not, in modern life, spending time on the floor, or crawling, this aspect of development is becoming neglected.

Through Jenny's work in this area we have become aware, when visiting different children in a range of settings and situations, that many young children seem to be sitting and moving about with clenched hands. This could be for various reasons. Here is one reason, first expressed by Elizabeth Harrison in 1895: 'The clenched hands denote the struggle within, and great artists often use them as the only marked sign of the inward turmoil which the calm face and strong will are determined to conceal. The open and extended palm indicates entire freedom from deceit or concealment' (Harrison, 1895: 166).

Spreading the hand out, and feeling feedback from the pressure of the fingers in a fist on the palm of the hand, is important for the later development of writing.

Finger rhymes also often offer possibilities for changing the focus, as with the two birds who sit on a wall then fly away. It is important to encourage children to track the finger with their eyes as the birds fly away.

Finger rhymes should not be used in isolation from other types of rhyme

Finger rhymes are part of a range of rhymes – from finger rhymes to action songs, nursery rhymes, and books of stories and information. Children need to experience finger rhymes alongside gross motor movements and the music, singing, use of three-dimensional objects, the rhythm and rhyme in order to help them become able to fine focus on the fingers. It is only the poetry cards and the locomotion action songs that are introduced later, for some children in Reception who are on the way to phonemic awareness, and in the first years of statutory education in the different countries of the UK.

The photographs in this chapter are from observations made at a nursery school in which children aged from two to five years were with a nursery teacher. The children came from different community and cultural groups, with some having an identified special need/disability as the intake for this nursery school came from across the city, depending upon parental choice and availability.

Note the clenching and opening out of the hands. Children who have clenched hands have probably not had sufficient experience of crawling, and may be tense, which then constrains the ability to learn. The pressure on the palm of the hand sends important signals to the brain, and this also aids the co-ordination of hand movements, vision and hearing

The teacher, having attended the training session, decided to use the proposed three stages to the finger rhymes and was amazed at what she found.

It is interesting that one of the rhymes the children enjoyed was 'The Beehive' (see page 79). This was created by Emile Poulsson in 1893, but based on the format of Froebel's finger plays, for one of the early kindergartens in the USA.

Stage 1

The important thing when selecting finger rhymes for this stage is that they should involve the whole hand and all ten fingers, opening and shutting. These were particularly popular and much loved by the children. It is important to have a set of core finger rhymes to share together so that the children become profi-cient in them as they are regularly repeated in a sustained way. These are just a few examples of possible finger rhymes to share with them:

Open, Shut Them

Open, shut them, Open, shut them,
Give a little clap.
Open, shut them, Open, shut them
Put them on your lap.

Creep them, creep them, creep them, creep them,
Right up to your chin, chin, chin,
Open wide your little mouth
(Hesitate)
But do not put them in.

The joy of anticipation is an important element. Being able to predict what comes next is a crucial part of fluent reading later on. This is an early rehearsal for this.

Sitting on the floor is important

It is important for the children to sit on the floor so they feel 'grounded'. This links with work on developmental movement practice (Jabadao) by Penny Greenland and her colleagues. As we have already seen earlier in this chapter, this connection with the floor is important as a reference point for the body. It is very hard for a young child to keep the midline and balance if they have to sit on a chair.

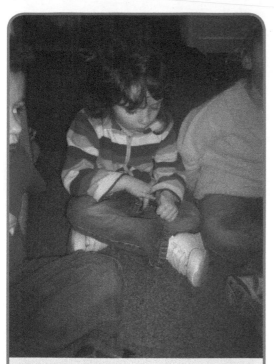
When concentrating hard and doing something very difficult, it is important not to rush children. Children need time to learn without pressure. It also takes time to get the fingers into position and to sing at the same time as doing so

Sing the finger rhyme very slowly

Children will be trying to focus on the detail, and they will need the adult to do the rhyme slowly so they can work it out. As with learning a foreign language it helps if people speak slowly.

The children in the group enjoyed these songs and found them easier than the next stage, when they had to isolate different fingers. It helped to talk about what was happening, such as asking them to squeeze their hands to look like a ball, and keep them still, and then lift one finger at a time. In other words, language which explains the mechanics of the movements (as Vygotsky, 1978, suggests) supported the way the children understood and were able to carry out the mechanics of the actions.

Ten Little Fingers
I have ten little fingers,
They all belong to me.
I can make them do things.
Would you like to see?
I can shut them up tight,
Open them wide.
I can put them together,
Or make them hide.
I can make them jump high,
Or make them go low.
I can fold them up quietly (fold arms),
And sit just so.

There is an early transition here into an action song with the folding of the arms.

What were the results (outcomes) for Stage 1 finger rhymes?

- The children were extending the palms of their hands more often in a variety of situations. Their hands were not so often clenched. Hands were more flexible.
- Children were helped to become more aware of the different sensations in their hands, when stretching their fingers and squeezing.
- The visual gaze at their hands was enhanced. They fixated on their fingers both close up and at arm's length.
- Getting to know themselves as physical beings was encouraged (what Penny Greenland calls the 'felt sense of living').
- Children enjoyed the sense of anticipation.

The teacher picked out the children's pleasure in anticipation as a key element in introducing finger rhymes at this early stage: 'The children feel a sense of anticipation for the word, waiting for their favourite word to come.' Prediction (having an idea of what is coming next) is a very important element of reading later on. Marie Clay (1998) argues this needs to be over 90% in fluent reading.

Stage 2

Go from whole hand to fingers

The important thing during this stage is to help children isolate the different fingers during the finger rhyme, and also help them to name each finger. Choose finger rhymes with this in mind.

In Stage 2 children have to isolate each finger, so this song is a bit more challenging than 'Ten Little Fingers' or 'Open, Shut Them', in Stage 1.

- Sitting on the floor is still important.
- So is singing the finger rhyme slowly.
- Talk about the position of the finger.
- Moving and talking about what and how you are moving will help children to succeed.

Tommy Thumb

Tommy thumb, Tommy thumb,
Where are you?
Here I am, Here I am, How do you do?

Peter pointer, Peter pointer
Where are you?
Here I am, Here I am, How do you do?

Toby tall, Toby tall
Where are you?
Here I am, Here I am, How do you do?

Ruby ring, Ruby ring
Where are you?
Here I am, Here I am, How do you do?

Baby small, Baby small
Where are you?
Here I am, Here I am, How do you do?

Fingers all, Fingers all,
Where are you?
Here we are, Here we are, How do you do?

Encourage children to look at both hands by doing so yourself as you sing

This kind of tracking is very important for later reading. When babies crawl they are looking from side to side of their midline while they are travelling, without moving their head, which is an important development. Later, when children read, they are tracking the line of print with their eyes, without moving their head from side to side. It is important to encourage children to watch their fingers.

Children find it fascinating to change their fingers in position. They like to have names for them, such as 'thumb', 'pointing finger', 'little finger', and so on. It is important to encourage children to use their fingers as symbols.

Walking, talking and pretending are important developments during the first three years. A symbol is something which stands for something else. An excellent way for young children to explore symbols is to let them see and understand that their own fingers can be made to stand for something else. Once they understand that each finger has a name (i.e. 'thumb', etc.), they will understand that they can also pretend that their thumb is a person (i.e. Tommy).

What were the results (outcomes) for Stage 2 finger rhymes?

- The teacher found that the children developed better control of their fingers (and so did the staff and parents!).
- Visual tracking improved.
- There was an increase in vocabulary.
- Children anticipated the words and finger movements.
- Although adults focussed on naming the fingers, the children began to see that they could use their fingers as symbols to represent characters in a story, which prepared them for Stage 3.

The teacher felt that it was at Stage 2 that she saw most difference, although all three stages were important. From the point of view of the **physical development and movement** encouraged through finger rhymes, she found that, as in Stage 1:

Both boys and girls enjoy finger rhymes. These help all children to engage in an experience which helps them on a good journey into literacy. It is important to sing rhymes slowly to give children time to get into position as well as to sing the words. It is also worthwhile to allow plenty of repetition so that they have enough time to develop their skills and consolidate them

sitting on the floor helped children to be comfortable, grounded and balanced. This enabled them to move the top part of their bodies with the bottom part feeing safe and secure. The children became aware of themselves and of their physicality, but had time to look and listen. It is a physical skill to focus closely on the fingers and then be able to focus beyond, as the hand is held up.

Although these are deeply important aspects of learning, perhaps the most exciting one was the way that children responded to the 'literature' elements involved. The teacher added: 'It is the "pantomime" – the senses are there in the background – which allows the child to develop his individual style, leading into free-flow play (Bruce, 1991). For boys the finger rhymes have led them to being interested in key stories.'

The links with **music** are also strong. The sound elements are crucial to learning to read later: 'It is the longer rhymes that children enjoy the most. They enjoy linking sound rhythm and beat to the phonic, but most of all they enjoy the anticipation and variety.'

The children also developed a sense of **drama**. 'The children change the identity of the fingers and their voices to represent the different fingers. They can be what they want them to be.'

A key feature of the finger rhymes was that of touch, which children do not experience when using finger puppets.

> It is the sense of touch in the different movements, supported by the looking that is important. The children refer to 'Ruby Ring' as the 'tricky one', but they can now hold 'Ruby Ring' up straight. They will often talk about what 'Ruby Ring' is doing while they are engaged in other activities, and practitioners will also ask the children, 'Can you see how your "Peter Pointer" is painting? Does it feel different with "Ruby Ring" or "Baby Small"? Is the sensation different?' The identity of 'Ruby Ring' is big!

So although Stage 2 was about isolating the fingers and naming them, the children quickly grasped the potential of using their separate fingers as symbols. They readily turned them into characters, and short narratives and storylines were soon developing around them. It is almost impossible to keep children in Stage 2 from going on to Stage 3. It is the adults only who need to keep these separate in their heads, to ensure children have a balance of each.

Stage 3

The finger rhymes help with whole body control, and vice versa

It is important not to introduce finger rhymes in isolation from action songs. These help each other, so children will need both. Gross motor movements are crucial in development and learning. The action songs in Stage 3 link gross motor with the fine motor finger rhymes, and act as a bridge between them. The hands are extended into larger movements of the arm. The gaze is also extended further from the body to look at the hand from a greater distance.

In later literacy development, children will need to have both good gross motor and fine motor skills. The gross shoulder movement controls the fine motor movements of the fingers, as anyone who has broken a shoulder and tried to write a letter to a friend will know!

Characters and stories using the fingers as symbols: nature, people and objects

We have based our collection of finger rhymes on the classification of Friedrich Froebel in his 'Mother Songs', using his categories of nature, people and objects.

This is a finger rhyme about nature:

Two Little Dicky Birds

Two little dicky birds, sitting on a wall.
One called Peter, one called Paul.
Fly away Peter, fly away Paul.
Come back Peter, come back Paul.

This is a finger rhyme about people:

Two Fat Gentlemen

Two fat gentlemen met in the lane,
Bowed most politely, bowed once again.
How do you do? How do you do?
How do you do again?

Two thin ladies met in the lane,
Bowed most politely, bowed once again.
How do you do? How do you do?
How do you do again?

Two tall policemen met in the lane,
Bowed most politely, bowed once again.
How do you do? How do you do?
How do you do again?

Two little schoolboys met in the lane,
Bowed most politely, bowed once again.
How do you do? How do you do?
How do you do again?

Two little babies met in the lane,
Bowed . . .

Practitioners have been impressed at the way children have enjoyed the longer rhymes. They liked the repetition and entered into the spirit of performing the song together.

The last category of finger rhymes involves objects:

The Beehive

Modern version:

Here is the beehive,
But where are the bees?
Hidden away
Where nobody sees.

Look and you'll see them
Come out of the hive,
One, two, three, four, five
BZZZZZZZZZZZZZZZZZ

Emilie Poulsson (an early Froebelian) – original version:

Here is the beehive.
Where are the bees?
Hidden away where nobody sees.
Soon they'll come creeping out of the hive –
One! – two! – three! – four! – five!

What were the results (outcomes) of Stage 3 finger rhymes?

- Gross and fine motor skills are linked.
- The gaze is extended.
- Characters and stories develop in simple, engaging ways.
- There was symbolic representation.
- Imagination developed (remember the example of the Spiderman finger rhyme created by the three year old boy?).
- They began to link the finger rhymes to stories.
- They developed a sense of pantomime and drama.

The teacher found that Stage 3 focussed on gross motor skills using the hands and fingers alongside the rest of the body in controlled movements. We began to realize that covering fingers with finger puppets undermined the learning, rather in the way that in the last chapter Trevarthen suggested that electronic toys, rather than play with a traditional soft ball, could undermine the interactions between baby and parent or key person. The noises toys make and the flashing lights or the covering of fingers by puppets, are what Bruner calls 'noisy cues' which are taking children away from the essentials of literacy. The teacher here noted:

The children enjoyed the finger rhymes without the puppets just as much.

This teacher who, with her colleagues, decided to explore finger rhymes as a result of the course she attended, said, 'It is Stage 3 in the finger rhymes that "grabs" practitioners, but it is probably the least important. Stage 2 is the most important, and Stage 1 is very necessary – it is an integral part of development at an early stage. It is finding out about the body – getting to know yourself as a physical being and that your finger looks the same here or there. It is a stage for exploring the senses. The body is feeling really comfortable – the children sit on the floor, so are "grounded" and this could be anywhere – indoors or outdoors.'

IN SUMMARY

In this chapter, we have looked at the important beginnings of multi-sensory learning on the journey into communication, language and literacy and how:

- the hands help adults and children to make meaning together through emotive gestures right from the start
- finger rhymes encourage parents and key persons to enjoy early literacy experiences with their children
- the songs using the hands develop the midline, tracking and focus, and the co-ordination of hand and eye in physical development, all crucial for later literacy
- they help children with fine motor skills and gross motor skills so that each helps the other along in ways which will support the development of writing
- finger rhymes are examples of early and engaging opportunities for the development of symbol making and symbol use by children just beginning to represent as they learn to walk, talk and pretend.

Key Terms

Phonemic awareness – becoming aware of and being able to identify the sounds in language

Phonological awareness – becoming aware of sounds in the language

Rhythm – a sequence of movements in time

Syllabification – breaking a word down into syllables, which are chunks of sound in a word (di-no-saur)

Symbol – one thing that stands for another

Reading

Matterson, E. (1991) *This Little Puffin: Finger Plays and Nursery Rhymes*. London: Puffin.

Further Reading

Malloch, S. and Trevarthen, C. (eds) (2010) *Communicative Musicality: Exploring the Basics of Human Companionship*. Oxford: Oxford University Press.

Chapter 5

Mark-Making and Writing

In this chapter we show how:

- reading and writing are processes which depend on each other;
- physical co-ordination is essential to reading and writing;
- children need caring people around them in order to develop fully, especially for symbolic development.

Mark-making

The marks children make – their first scribble drawings – are the beginnings of the essentials they need in order to write.

Scribble drawing. 'We were all drawing pictures, after singing "Row your Boat" and songs on the way to school. Paige (16 months) wanted to draw and drew this picture'

27/2/06
Loui drew a picture of a duck. Well he drew a shape and said look duck. We then got out my ducks and sang 5 little ducks went swimming one day see obs.

'Loui drew a picture of a duck. Well, he drew a shape and said, "Look, duck!" We then got out my ducks and sang "Five Little Ducks went Swimming One Day".' Children often look at their scribbles and see imaginable likenesses in them

The childminder reported that:

Each time a duck swam away, I hid it under my skirt. Loui loved this and said, 'Where duck gone?' I showed him it was under my skirt. Loui liked this idea and when the next duck swam away he hid it up his trouser leg. Lizzie did the same with her duck, and the last duck she hid up her top. We all laughed as this was very funny. We managed to get all the ducks back out for the last part of the song when all the ducks return.

Lizzie was able to sing the bits of the song I missed out, e.g. I sang 'Five little ducks went … ' And Lizzie would sing 'swimming one day over the hills and far away'. I sang, 'Mother duck said … ' and again Lizzie would sing 'quack, quack, quack, quack' and we all joined in with the 'four little ducks came swimming back'. I wrote the words of the song in front of the children and Loui said, 'Julie you writing.' I answered, 'Yes, I am writing.'

Once I had finished writing the words, Lizzie followed them with her finger across the page from left to right as she sang the whole song by herself. Loui also had a go at following the words with his finger and he moved his finger in a circle motion over the words as Lizzie and I sang the words of the song.

Here we can see, using play props, a rehearsal for segmenting and blending (separate ducks, or ducks altogether on the pond). We can also see an understanding from Lizzie that print represents meaning, and the glimmerings of this same realization in Paige. The children can see that what they sing can be written down, and Lizzie has gained the understanding that it is possible to read back what you have just written down. Reading and writing cannot be separated. What we encode we also decode.

Paige is discovering mark-making. Loui and Lizzie are beginning to see and understand that they can be symbol makers. They can do this through painting or drawing.

Personal symbols are a bridge across to shared, conventional symbols

In the 1930s Vygotsky identified the way that children's drawings develop. Early letters appear in them, and are gradually pushed out to the edge, to become emergent writing.

The important thing in Stage 1 nursery rhymes is to enjoy these with children, to act them out, and to leave play props and small world and books so that they can revisit and try them out in their own time as they wish (see Chapter 2). Rhymes build on what is natural to children, and so we, as adults, need to use them in ways which enhance this

Children will begin to give meaning to what they 'write' and to realize that there is a relationship between how letters and words sound and look. The child is beginning to establish that print represents meaning in books, and that you can actually make your own print! Marie Clay wrote a very important book on this topic in 1975 called *What Did I Write?* Realizing that someone else can read what you have written is one of the most exciting moments in a child's life. Ferreiro (1983; 1997) found from observation in different countries that were Spanish and English speaking, that children would spontaneously begin to 'write' by typically using between two and five symbols to indicate a word, and long lines of curves or zig zags to indicate sentences.

There are layers in the way that our understanding of print develops. We can see this in the way Loui began his journey into literacy:

- Layer 1 – The toy ducks are objects that carry the meanings around the experiences the children have had of seeing them in the park, and singing the song with Julie.
- Layer 2 – His drawing of the duck was not intentional, but having scribbled, Loui thought it reminded him of the duck. This was an imagal likeness of a duck.
- Layer 3 – Loui will begin intentionally to draw a duck.
- Layer 4 – Loui will write marks of his own as 'writing' the word 'duck'.
- Layer 5 – Loui will begin to use conventional letters to make the word 'duck'.

Here Piaget helps us to value the personal symbols children make. These are the bridge between:

- objects holding meaning (the toy duck as part of the much-loved song, and the drawing of the duck Loui has made)
- symbols the child makes marks on paper. Loui did not set out to draw a duck, but the marks he made became a personal symbol that held meaning for him.

Bialystok (1991: 78) says objects (like the toy ducks the children use in the song) are imbued with meaning for each child. Loui's drawing was an object that was full of meaning for him.

However, the letters of the alphabet were not full of meaning for him, except for the letters of his own name. These alphabet letters were not personal objects. They were shared symbols representing shared meaning. This meant they did not hold personal meanings.

When he was four years old, Loui's mother suggested he might write a 'thank you' card for Julie, and went to find one. While she was gone, he wrote on a piece of paper, 'J'. After a pause, he added, 'uli', thus writing 'Julie'. His mother was thrilled. He said it was like his name (which had the letters 'u', 'l' and 'i'). He had understood that letters were symbols that represented meanings (e.g. Julie's name).

Amanda began to write the 'A' for Amanda. Her family were thrilled. A few weeks later she started to write the letter on its side. When asked why, she replied, 'I've fallen over.' The letter was still a personal object for her, and did not yet represent shared meaning. This does not yet treat a letter as a cultural convention.

Conversations are between people. They are immediate and full of thoughts and feelings. We often do not meet the people who write to us or write books

It is very important to understand, as Margaret Donaldson (1978: 178) reminds us, that writing is often remote. We see the person reading to us, talking to us, writing a shopping list or an invitation, or we find out information for ourselves. But the person who writes a book or poem is more often than not unknown to us.

This is why shopping lists, messages and greetings cards written in the presence of children are important everyday situations where they can see people writing and realize that what we say, think, and feel can be written down.

The importance of names

A child's name will usually be the first fixed string of letters to be written spontaneously as a word. This is because of the emotional element. That name is part of a child's identity.

However, we need to sound a note of caution here. Children are able to respond to being called different names in different contexts with different people there are cultural variations in this too. Often, children have formal names and family names. These will be used in different situations and contexts.

Margaret Donaldson (1978) points out that when our learning makes human sense to us, we are able to tackle some quite abstract ideas. She says that one way in which learning becomes meaningless is to put children in a context-free situation. They will then import their own ideas in order to create meaning, based on what makes human sense.

To read and write, 'It is necessary to become skilled in manipulating systems and in abstracting forms and patterns' (Donaldson, in ECP, 2005, in Bruce, 2005a: 18). She points out that things like engineering depend on being able to

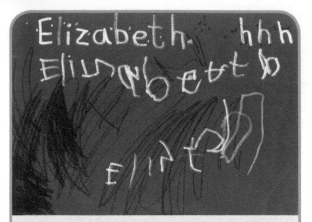

Lizzie has asked the childminder to write her name for her. She has managed to copy, underneath, the first three letters, 'Eli', but the 'z' is a challenge as it involves a more complex formation. She has a go. The lower case 'a' is difficult, but she does not give up. Her name is a long and difficult one to write. We need to bear this in mind when we make blanket requirements on all children to write their names by the time they begin statutory education. It is easier to write 'Tom' than 'Elizabeth'. Elizabeth decides to experiment with the letter 'h' in the right-hand corner, with 'z' placed underneath. It is important that she is given opportunities to enjoy this and not to be put under pressure

function in a real world with the support of familiar events: 'disembedded thinking, although by definition it calls for the ability to stand back from life, yields its greatest riches when it is conjoined with doing' (Donaldson, in ECP, 2005, in Bruce, 2005a: 18).

Children are natural problem-solvers and problem-generators (Karmiloff-Smith, 1992), because they are human. The brain embraces problem-solving. There is now a wealth of research literature that shows the way in which children will tease out how to write down the words they hear (Bissex, 1980; Ferreiro, 1997). The Basic Skills Agency (2005) have written a modern-day summary that builds on the edifice created by research and presents this in a way that is accessible to parents.

In order to write in conventional terms, children need to:

- work out the phoneme/grapheme links (to link sounds and letters)
- be able to segment and blend, blend and segment
- begin to see that these are placed in words
- see how words are placed in sentences.

Yet this does not mean that children cannot write, or have a go at writing, until all of these things are in place. Writing is one of those marvellous areas of development and learning where we find out and understand as we go. Children writing in English need this natural problem-solving approach to writing – which is fortunately part of our human brain function – more than children writing in other languages. This is because English is one of the most irregular languages in the world.

English as one of the most irregular languages in the world

George has to learn that although his name sounds as if it starts with a 'J', it in fact starts with a 'G'. What sound can we hear at the start of **Shannon**? **Sian**? **Sean**? **Charlotte**? The sound is the same, but the written form is different in each of these. As Richard Feynman (1990), the Nobel Prize-winning physicist, said, 'The thing that doesn't fit is the most interesting.'

Lucy has spontaneously copied the words of the poem onto four pages. She has then added 'by Lucy' independently on the front cover. She is becoming aware that there are conventions in the way things are written down. She wants to participate in this. She finds it helpful to copy a well-known and loved nursery rhyme, 'To Market, To Market to Buy a Fat Pig', but she also enjoys the thrill of writing what she can by herself, independently of any assistance

*Children and adults use what they know to find out
what they don't know*

Lucy is four years old and is at her pre-school playgroup. She wants to write out
the poetry card, 'To market, to market to buy a fat pig'.

There are several important things here:

- She can use what she knows to write independently. She has learnt to write 'by'
  via all the drawings and paintings she has labelled as her own.
- We recognize irregular words more easily when they have emotional meaning
  for us. This is the case with our names and also with words like 'love' or 'dinosaur'. As Marian Whitehead points out, it is difficult to fall in love with words
  like 'to', 'the' or 'go'. On the other hand the word 'no' might well have more
  meaning as it is bathed in emotion and personal meanings!
- Lucy can write her own name independently. This has been a huge boost to her
  confidence and well-being. Finding she can write even a small part of what she
  wanted to say has encouraged her to keep going, and believe in herself as a writer.
- The leading teacher discusses Lucy's writing with the practitioners in the pre-
  school and the leader of the early years pedagogy team. They all agree that
  Lucy 'understands the purpose of print as well as an appreciation of how
  books work. Her letter formation is accurate and clear and she is beginning to
  space each word appropriately'.

Adults who set copying tasks for children are not helpful

Dreary exercises in copying are a waste of time as well as demoralizing. Tracing
words is even less helpful, and gives children the message 'you cannot do this, so
you had better trace the letters'.

But many children will want to copy quite naturally. Lucy, for example, is trying
to feel the flow of the words and capture the syntax. She is beginning to understand that writing is made up of flow and sentences. The syntax is the order of
the words as they are spoken, and then keeping the same order as the words are
written down (Mallett, 2005).

Writing her name, which she does not need to copy, means Lucy has taken
a small, fixed string of letters and made them into a word. She has managed this
on her own. She has needed to learn this as sight vocabulary, as the phoneme–
grapheme link in 'L-u-cy' is not obvious. But this is so with much of the English language. It is full of irregularities in the way it sounds and also in the way it is written.

In copying a poetry card she is taking on the challenge of a much longer fixed
string – the sentences making up the words of a rhyme. But in this way she is
beginning to sort out letters, words and sentences, although she does not know
it yet and cannot talk about it. Understanding comes before competence and performance in writing, as well as before every aspect of learning. Marie Clay emphasizes the importance of working out the differences between a letter, word and

sentence. Through their experiments with writing, children begin to work this out, helped by adults and other children in their cultural community.

It helps to look at drawings and writing together

The group of practitioners looking at Lucy's drawing and writing shared what they were thinking with Lucy's parents. The practitioners were impressed with the way she had added detail to the leaf, and stripes on the jumper. She had demonstrated a 'core and radial' schema with the head and hair, the flower and the pig. She had an open semicircle in her drawing which was a typical indication of readiness for independent efforts at writing, and she was beginning to do this. Her drawings and the independent writing of her name suggested to the practitioners that she is making good progress, and that she is becoming confident and developing the necessary skills to become an independent writer.

Where does the alphabet come in?

We can see that learning the alphabet is of limited use to Lucy at this point in her development and learning, but learning the names of the letters in her name will be a useful and emotionally engaging start. Names of letters should always be learnt in the context of written words, rhymes, poems, stories and environmental notices and messages. This is because the name of each letter is not about the sound. A letter name is a general name, which does not change. On the other hand, the 'e' in 'egg' sounds completely different to the sound of the 'e' in 'eel'. Letter names are a constant in a world of changing phonemes/graphemes and therefore act as anchors.

This links with Loui, mentioned earlier in the chapter, who was writing a card for his childminder. Jeni Riley points out how studies that focussed on teaching 'the alphabet by rote, had no enduring value and this fails to guarantee an early successful start to reading. The appreciation of the symbolic representation of letters for spoken sounds occurs slowly over time and with exposure to meaningful experiences of print and text' (Riley, 1999: 58).

Since the days of John Locke's alphabet blocks, and probably before, children have delighted in letter names. When Lucy points at the letter 'L' on a car with 'L' plates and says 'That's my name!', we might say something along the lines of

Skye finds the sound 'S' as in Skye. The children enjoy the garden alphabet, and spontaneously think of words starting with each sound. Ollie said, 'H – Humza'. He thought a moment and then said, 'Happy, hug, hurry up – hurry up and do it! HOG!'

In the top photo a boy has written his name on the flagstones in chalk. He often returns to his name and stands on it. He and his friend make a game. The rule is to stand on your name, and then run around the garden for a bit, shouting 'here we go' on the run, and then to suddenly make a dash and return to the name, and stand together on it. A child's name carries a huge and lasting meaning and is central in learning to read and write

In the photograph underneath, the boy writes his name on the flagstones in chalk. He never goes to the writing table indoors, but he engages in writing his name in this way, and on different days he writes his name with a paintbrush and bucket of water on the tarmac area outside

'Yes, that's the letter 'L' (pronounced "el"). In your name it sounds "Le", L-u-cy'.

If we do not respond, we are, in Marie Clay's (1998) view, rejecting Lucy's literacy understanding rather than building on it. In the same way, Loui picked out the letters in Julie's name that were the same as his, but may not have been mapping the sounds onto the letters (the phoneme/graphemes link) at that point.

Chanting the alphabet is only useful when you are already familiar with how it works. Therefore is useful, with six- and seven-year-olds, to sing alphabet songs.

Writing does not always have to be on paper

In the photographs you can see boys mark-making in relation to their names on the flagstones in the garden. This is significant. Boys often do not enjoy mark-making on paper as much as girls do. They seem to be echoing some of the graphic forms in their own spontaneous mark-making near where the adult has written names.

Although most of the settings, as one practitioner describes it, offer children 'a wide range of activities and resources to promote mark-making and encourage the children to experiment with their own writings and labelling ... there is more interest shown by boys this year'.

Boys responded to the three-dimensional, movement-packed opportunities for mark-making and writing. In the photograph on page 92 you can see a boy quietly engaged in watching the practitioner writing the rhyme 'Humpty Dumpty' on the ground outside. He was very familiar with the rhyme, having actively played with props and taken part in a large-scale drama of the rhyme. Boys often prefer to be outside as they learn.

Going with nature and not against it – helping boys to engage with writing

It is enjoyable for young children to 'write' using plastic letters, and the keyboards of computers can be very attractive to them as well. However, as Blakemore and Frith (2005) point out, if children are to write with pencils and paper, they will need to be able to co-ordinate their fingers. The motor cortex, which controls hand/finger co-ordination, is not usually matured and developed in this respect until a child is at least five years of age. This also comes later in boys than in girls. Many of the boys we worked with were summer-born babies. These findings, emphasizing physical maturation and co-ordination, have far-reaching implications for four-year-olds in Reception classes.

Sarah-Jayne Blakemore and Uta Frith (2005: 71) suggest that the letter shapes most used today are Roman in origin, and thus well suited to stone inscriptions – but not so well suited to writing and reading in real life! Some of the letters are also mirror-reversible, which makes them confusing.

b ... d
p ... q

If we think of these as solid objects in a three-dimensional world, we can twist them around and see they are the same shapes. It is only when these are placed onto two-dimensional paper that we are unable to twist them, and so they have to be written in a certain spatial relationship: 'The mappings between symbols and speech have to be learned, and this learning has a lasting impact on the brain' (Blakemore and Frith, 2005: 71).

Children are very observant, and they are willing participators in the community if given support and encouragement to do so. One of the children has noticed that the adults have labelled the places in the organic garden where the plants have been placed. Here we can see his/her experimenting with writing a label for the organic garden

This writing area has been carefully set up to attract and engage both boys and girls. It is not overcrowded in its provision. Everything has a place, so it is easy to keep tidy. Children are free to use it, and it has privacy in that it faces the wall, which encourages concentration when a child is mark-making or experimenting with writing

The boy is watching the adult writing the rhyme 'Humpty Dumpty' on the ground outside. Adults perform an important role when they scribe for children. If the adult says the word as they write it, this helps children to hear the syllables and to develop sight vocabularies

People who can read are decoding words automatically, even if they have no intention of reading the word. Stroop (in Blakemore and Frith, 2005) presented people with lists of words written in different colours, and asked them to name the colour of each word. Some of the words were also the names of colours –

Blue.
Purple.

It took people longer to read these: 'This is because before you name the colour of the ink you involuntarily read the word, and the meaning comes to mind unbidden. Once you have learned to read, you cannot help but read the meaning of the words' (Blakemore and Frith, 2005: 71–2). A child who has reached the stage of being an automatic reader can do two things at the same time:

- identify whole words
- translate the letters into sounds.

A large European collaborative study, using brain-scanning techniques, by neuroscientists Paulesu, Demonet and Frith (in Blakemore and Frith, 2005), points out that a reader uses one or other of three areas of the brain. But they will lean a little more heavily on some more than others, depending on the writing system used. This fits in with findings by Goswami: 'When learning to read English or French, more work is done by the region of the brain responsible for whole word recognition. When learning to read Italian, more work is done by the region that is responsible for letter-sound translation' (Blakemore and Frith, 2005: 79).

Getting the idea of flow in writing

Practitioners in one of the settings mentioned above had been particularly interested in the way that reading and writing were intertwined.

They often scribed for children when they wanted to retell a story that had been read to them previously. This is the story Rhianna (four years and four months) retold:

The Elves and the Shoemaker

One day there was a shoemaker and his wife. They was very poor.

He cut some shoes and left them on the workbench. He was surprised to see some shoes but he didn't know who did sew them. So a rich lady came and put shoes on. She said they were perfect.

She gave the shoemaker a big bag of money. He cut two pairs of shoes and left them on the bench.

A rich man came into the shops. He said, 'I'll take both pairs.' He gave the shoemaker two big bags of money.

Every time he found perfect shoes on his workbench, he cut shoes out and left them on his workbench.

They hide in a cupboard. Two elves went in, the clothes were really old. They made some shoes. The wife saw the old clothes and made tiny new ones ready.

Next time, 'We like our clothes,' said the elves.

'We like our shoes,' said the wife.

The end

The practitioner wrote: 'Rhianna knew I was scribing her story, and waited after retelling a page of the story for me to catch up on my writing. She can write her name clearly and fluently.'

Both Lucy and Rhianna can write their names independently, and a few other words that they are proud to be able to do. But because the adult would write down what they wanted to say, they are spared the frustration of not being able to write whole chunks independently. They only wrote what they could manage:

- Lucy used a poetry card to copy words she could not write independently.
- The adult provided a rich literacy environment as part of the enabling environment.
- Rhianna had found a helpful adult to scribe the retelling of the story.

We found in every setting that the child's name was emotionally important and usually the first word they wrote. (We saw in an earlier chapter that Sylvia Ashton-Warner pioneered the importance of words packed with feelings.)

David Crystal (2006: 167–9) reported on the British Council's (2004) world survey of what he calls 'wordmelodies'. These either sound beautiful ('blossom', 'lullaby', 'kangaroo') or mean something beautiful ('mother', 'eternity').

Emotionally important words are the stuff of creative writing and poetry making (Barrs and Meek, 2007). We did not want to neglect this aspect of writing, but it is a sad reflection of the way most children are currently taught to read and write that they do not become lifelong writers for the sheer pleasure of it. Writing takes huge effort, but it should be a worthwhile and satisfying effort. It should also foster creative energy and give it space to blossom. As Beatrix Potter (1974, in Pearce, in Meek et al., 1977) said, 'There's something delicious about writing the first words of a story. You never quite know where it will take you.'

Children often want to write their name on the models they make. This often develops so that they will wish to write about the model as their technical and mechanical understanding of what is involved in writing develops. Boys will often prefer to write about a three-dimensional structure they have made. This gives them memory hooks to structure their writing around, and is like a concrete 'story'. However, not all children enjoy creating fiction stories. Some will prefer to write about real things

Some adult writers structure a story before they begin to write, but many do not. Philip Pullman believes that the characters, out of the shadows, should grab the writer and take them somewhere. This was so for Philippa Pearce when she wrote *A Dog so Small.* (in Meek et al., 1977: 182): 'From the very beginning – perhaps even before you think of writing a story at all – the story must *grow*. An idea grows in your mind as a tree grows from a seed. The idea of the story is the seed, and it grows with the slowness of natural growth.' She was anxious that the technical making of the story (transcribing) and the structuring of it (beginning, middle, end, etc.) should not get in the way of composing the story. She favoured just getting it down on paper, and then tidying it up afterwards. The characters and the storying should be at the forefront. What we want to say is the most important thing. How we write it must come second, as every writer will tell you. Adults working with children need to remember this, so that they can fully support children on their journey into literacy.

From a three-dimensional world to a two-dimensional world

What happens before children reach the point where they are trying to write their name and other emotionally important words?

Loui, at two years and six months old, gives us some clues here (see his drawing on page 95). His childminder wrote about his drawing:

> After playing 'Row, Row, Row your Boat', we did some drawing. Loui said 'Julie Boat.' I said, 'Just like the song "Row, Row your Boat".' Loui said, 'Draw crocodile, draw crocodile,' holding out his pen. I drew the crocodile. Loui covered over his eyes and teeth. 'Where boat gone?' said Loui. Then he said, 'Where crocodile gone?' I asked, 'Is it hiding?' Loui said, 'No – gone.'

It is useful to unpick this. From about five or so months old until age two or three children are fascinated by peekaboo games. This is about all sorts of things, but one of them concerns the way they are sorting out that people and objects can be placed over or behind each other. At first it will seem that someone has disappeared, but they are still there behind a cloth.

They seem to be saying two things – a person and a cloth or curtain – cannot both occupy the same space, so what is happening here? Has the person gone away? No, they are still there!

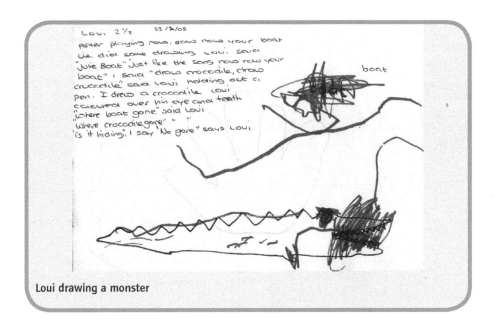

Loui drawing a monster

Piaget (1962) describes this as developing the permanence of an object. As this becomes established delight in the game seems to increase, and toddlers love to 'play' with permanence.

Walking, talking and pretending

Walking, talking and pretending come together in a wonderful cluster, with far-reaching consequences for the development and learning of the child.

Loui has reached this point. He now understands that you can take a three-dimensional thing (in this case a crocodile) and draw it. Just as Rhianna needed someone else to scribe for her, he needs someone to draw the crocodile. He then does what he can manage, which is to cover the crocodile. He does this by colouring over it. He plays with the idea of something hiding or gone (the concept of permanence). It is safer to make the crocodile disappear! Emotion is always there when we work with young children.

This is a rehearsal for putting words – which are three-dimensional sounds – into two-dimensional graphemes. Loui is on the literacy journey towards selecting the right symbols for the situation.

This is Daddy. He has really long legs. He is the biggest. Daddy's hair goes all the way round. He looks like a lion. Mummy is Middle. She has lots of long hair and long legs. Hannah looks like a penguin. I will give her only one eye and hair. Penguins do have hair. These are Philip's legs. They are really long. I will put his head at the bottom. I have eyes, eye-lashes, nose, mouth, hair and ears. I'm the smallest

Templates and colouring in outlines: damaging the journey into writing

Piaget (1962) talks about the importance of personal symbols as the beginnings of writing. Drawings are often not recognizable in what they represent, but they are representational nevertheless.

We need to encourage children to make personal symbols. These act as a bridge to the conventional symbols that make up written texts.

John Matthews (2003) argues that children benefit from adults helping them in their early attempts to do this, but it is unhelpful to give out templates or to require them to colour in outlines. That gives a child the message 'You can't draw! So you had better use this drawing instead of doing your own'.

From personal symbols towards real writing

Lizzie has travelled further in her journey into writing than Loui, but she is three years and seven months old. She has been interested in her family of late, and whether she will still be Lizzie when she grows up.

We can see Loui has benefitted from an older child drawing independently and with confidence and pleasure alongside him. Mixing the ages of children is a very positive thing. Older children love to show younger children how they do things, and explain these, and younger children can see what lies ahead without the pressure to perform.

Is it significant that Lizzie refered to mummy as 'Middle'? She had been singing the finger rhyme 'Peter Pointer' with the childminder. It may well be that she was using the analogy of her fingers and their names to look at the heights of people in her family. Goswami (1998) points out that children use analogies as a powerful tool for thinking.

Jeni Riley (2007: 81) emphasizes the importance of an enabling environment indoors and outdoors as a general backcloth to reading and writing, with continuity in the provision of a rich, broad and deep language and literacy environment throughout early childhood and through to seven years.

Forming letters

Children find capital letters easier at first. This is because they contain more lines and circular enclosures than curves. Parents are often accused of teaching their children capital letters, and criticized for it. In fact children very sensibly select only what they can manage to write. Once they can draw a curve, they are in a position to take on lower case letters as they write (Bruce, 2005b: 2011, in press). This will often show in their drawings. Typically they will draw smiling and sad faces with an open semi-circle for the mouth. Eyebrows appear, and semi-circular ears. A boy whose father was a butcher who had his own shop drew a horizontal line with semi-circles along it. These were hooks to hang the meat on. In the drawing done by Lucy included in this chapter ('To market, To market to buy a fat pig', page 87) there are many open semi-circles, and by these she is quite naturally demonstrating that she is ready for writing in a lower case.

KEY MESSAGES ABOUT CHILDREN BEGINNING TO WRITE

- Writing draws on language, thoughts, feelings and relationships, but it is more distanced and remote than talking with people.
- Children need to know what writing is about, and what it is for, while surrounded by people who enjoy and take writing as a serious pleasure.
- Having something you want to say in writing (composing) is different from the mechanics of writing and forming letters (transcribing). Composing must not be dragged into the technical structuring of a story. Composing should flow. If a young child has never experienced flow, they will not enjoy writing later on. Most adults today will have missed out on this experience, through an over-emphasis on structuring and transcribing in their education in the early years.
- Early finger rhymes help the physical aspects of writing to develop. They enhance our biological development.
- Larger movements with the shoulders and whole body are also important (see Chapters 6 and 2 on action songs and enabling learning environments).
- Handwriting is not writing. Handwriting is how the letters are formed. Until children are spontaneously producing the open semi-circle in their drawings and mark-making, it is not appropriate to formally teach them lower case letter formation. However they will often enjoy building words with loose alphabets.
- Children should not be pressured into writing before the motor cortex is sufficiently mature, but they should experience enabling environments, with positive relationships that respect them as the unique people they are. As practitioners who are working with other people's children we need to acquire and update the subject knowledge involved in the mechanics of writing, and the creativity, information and pleasure this brings.

Key Terms

Composing – this concerns having an idea on what you want to write about, which is usually best if not too prestructured in advance, and emerging instead as a story grows or an idea develops so that it doesn't vanish in the mechanics of the making

Fixed string – children need to understand that a word is made up of letters that are in a particular and unchangeable order and can be repeated over and over again. A child's name is usually the first fixed string they will engage with, because it is imbued with emotional and personal meaning for them

Grapheme – this is the cluster of letters that makes a sound, such as 'ch' in 'chip'

Phoneme – this is the smallest unit of sound in the language, such as 'ea' in the word 'tea'

Structuring – this means sorting out aspects such as the beginning, middle and end of a story, or idea

Syntax – this concerns the order of words when they are spoken

Transcribing – this involves children in the mechanics of writing, so it is about letter formation and the spacing between words, etc.

Reading

Hall, N. and Robinson, A. (2003) *Exploring Writing and Play in the Early Years* (2nd edn). London: David Fulton.

Further Reading

Whitehead, M. (2009) *Supporting Language and Literacy Development in the Early Years* (2nd edn). Maidenhead: Open University/McGraw-Hill Education.

Chapter **6**

Action Songs – On the Spot

In this chapter we show how:

- action songs are important;
- there are different types of action songs;
- action songs have a tradition;
- action songs are for moving different parts of the body.

Who started the tradition of singing action songs with children?

Friedrich Froebel, who was born in 1782 and died in 1852, pioneered action songs as well as finger rhymes and our understanding of the importance educationally of singing to babies. His influence, though not many people would realize this, continues in the action songs we sing daily with children. In Chapter 4 we focussed on finger rhymes, looking at the contribution they still make to today's practice. Froebel gave women status as educators of young children. During the time he was working, women were not regarded as having the physical stamina to teach. It was even thought that too much thinking might make them ill. Middle-class women were not expected to work and their role was as wives and mothers. Poorer women were often illiterate, and at this time literacy was not encouraged in the working classes as it was feared that this might lead to revolution.

Froebel created his 'Mother Songs' which involved singing to babies, and finger rhymes. Most of these are now very dated, but a few have remained as firm favourites, such as 'Pat a Cake, Pat a Cake, Baker's Man, Bake me a Cake as Fast as you Can'. As we saw in the chapters on parent/baby songs and finger rhymes, Froebel developed these in carefully thought-out ways, based on his observations of children and how mothers sang to them. It was the same with action songs.

He established the first training college for women to become teachers of young children. In Germany, where he lived, when he first suggested the idea in a lecture he was giving he was boo-ed by his audience because it was widely held that only men could be teachers. When his schools were closed by the Duke of Saxony in 1851 (a year before Froebel died), some people who could see the value of his work, and having left Saxony because of its oppressive regime, began to spread his ideas, and gradually the kindergartens he had first developed in Bad Blandenburg became part of England's education system for privileged children. This gave middle-class mothers, tied to their homes and domestic life, the opportunity to train locally through their accreditation with the National Froebel Foundation. The early English kindergartens were therefore home based, so that wives had to have the permission of their husbands to teach. This was to prove a major contribution to the emancipation of women. Others then took up the Froebelian approach in teaching the more vulnerable and less privileged children, through the development of free nursery schools in poor areas and especially in Edinburgh in Scotland. Margaret McMillan was a Scottish Froebel-influenced pioneer who pioneered the nursery schools with their emphasis on the garden and indoor and outdoor learning and play being at the heart of young children's education. These nursery schools grew up in large cities such as Edinburgh, London and Manchester.

Many of the central pillars of early childhood education were pioneered by Froebel. He emphasized learning through nature; physical movement and learning through the senses; the importance of play; community; and the central place of parents in a child's education. He also emphasized that young children need mature, highly trained and well educated teachers. He would doubtless have agreed with the African saying that it takes a whole village to bring up and educate a child. He felt that parents should not be left isolated and unsupported in bringing up their children. He valued mathematics and the arts, including dance, music, three-dimensional art, two-dimensional art, drama and literature, and felt that children should be introduced to understanding time (history) and space (geography) in ways that would engage their interest. He also designed educational wooden blocks, which he called the Gifts, and used materials such as clay, shape boards, pin boards, and early construction kits, which he called the Occupations (Bruce, in Miller and Pound, 2010).

Froebel's contribution still continues, and this is explored elsewhere (see Bruce, 2005; 2010; 2011). However, in this book, we have focussed on the movement games and 'Mother Songs' and have located their value, in an updated form, in current practice. Here 'Mother Songs' have become Together Songs. 'Finger Plays' have become known as Finger Rhymes. Movement games are described nowadays as Action Songs.

Why does the tradition continue today? Is it still a valuable tradition?

Action songs encourage creativity, memory, sensitivity to others, co-ordinated movement, communication, an increased vocabulary, language development, music, dance and drama, as well as sequencing, predicting and an awareness of detail and anticipation.

However, because this book is about the essentials of literacy – and each child's journey into literacy – both this chapter and Chapter 7 emphasize the way that action songs help with:

- using the body as a symbol
- listening to rhyming patterns
- appreciating the traditional canon of rhymes in the English language
- co-ordinating body movements while singing
- the links between gross and fine motor skills
- the use of the body as a musical instrument, connecting and co-ordinating different parts of the brain
- phonological awareness
- rhythm
- rhyme
- alliteration
- sequencing
- extending the gaze from tracking to a fine, fixed focus on detail.

The upper body: non-locomotion action songs

Feeling grounded and keeping the midline

In Chapter 3 on parent/baby songs, we explored the co-ordinated use of hands, eyes and hearing, which is important for children's later reading and writing.

Being grounded on the floor, stable, balanced and with the midline, is important when singing and moving to action songs using the upper body. This helps children co-ordinate the upper part of their bodies sufficiently so they may perform the actions (Kuhlman and Schweinhart, 1999).

The links between gross and fine motor movements

Children need both of these. That is what we mean by a rich, enabling, multi-sensory learning environment for developing their learning in their unique journeys into literacy. This is given emphasis in government frameworks for early childhood education in the UK.

Action songs help children to become symbol users

When children – even very young children who are just beginning to walk, talk and pretend – are introduced to action songs, they begin to understand that one thing can be made to stand for another.

Children with hearing impairments are helped, as they begin to learn signs together with the spoken language which is more challenging for them. This signing then helps the spoken language along.

Children with visual impairments also enjoy the movements, and this helps with their ability to locate their own body in space, and to develop better mobility. It is very challenging for a child who cannot see to progress from on-the-spot action songs to locomotion action songs, with upper and lower body co-ordinating. (This is explored in the next chapter.) Mobility presents great difficulty for children with visual impairment.

Holding a steady beat is important for developing the essentials of literacy and for life as a whole

Action songs help children to co-ordinate their upper and lower body in movement and song so they learn to locate themselves and their personal tempo in relation to the sounds, tunes, words and movements of others. Holding a steady beat is part of this.

Holding a steady beat (Bayley and Broadbent, 2004) is important in developing sensitivity of communication, in hearing the sounds, tones and rhythms of language needed for literacy. It is also required in music, dance, drama, sport, and life in general. Penny Greenland (2010) describes this in relation to the 'felt sense of self' in the movements of the body.

Keeping a steady beat

Research (Ellis, 1992) shows that young children vary in their responses to a steady beat. These include:

- patting knees with both hands
- clapping
- patting knees with alternate hands
- patting a knee with the preferred hand
- patting a knee with the non-preferred hand
- stepping to the toe and stepping back
- walking on the spot.

We all have a natural and personal tempo: 'This personal "timing" is the natural tempo at which the individual relates and reacts to the world' (Kuhlman and Schweinhart, 1999: 14).

It is easier for young children to keep a steady beat when the tempo is at or near their personal tempo

Children aged three to nine years will find it easier to keep a steady beat to a faster tune than when a tune is slow: 'The task of synchronising movement with music played slower than an individual's personal tempo is more difficult for that individual than the task of synchronising movement with music played faster than the individual's personal tempo' (Walter, in Kuhlman and Schweinhart, 1999: 3).

Head to feet – the order in which the brain develops co-ordinated movement

Co-ordinating the upper and lower body movements while singing or chanting

In their paper, Kuhlman and Schweinhart gathered together a range of research suggesting that children with poor control of their legs and feet (tripping and clumsy) often have incomplete cephalocaudal motor development. This means their upper body movements are more developed than their lower body movements, and the two are not well co-ordinated.

Young children, because of their point of biological maturation and development, will find it easier to use their upper body. They will need plenty of opportunities to do this. Action songs while sitting or standing on the spot help this along. These are important from the time a child can walk until they are seven years old. They tend to be sung at a fast tempo, which fits in with the natural tempo of most young children.

Because the co-ordination of movements of the upper body develops earlier than the lower body (Kuhlman and Schweinhart, 1999), children at the end of the *Early Years Foundation Stage* will not always have the same personal tempo in their top and bottom halves.

They may well be beginning to be able to clap to the fast or slow beat of an action song with success, holding the beat steady. This is because the upper body is becoming

Dressing-up clothes help to create the right atmosphere, and help children to take on a character and identify with the narrative (the story)

more co-ordinated. But they might need a faster song if they are asked to move about, because their feet and legs cannot slow down while holding a steady beat and step.

The body is the first musical instrument

Children who learn to play musical instruments later on are at an advantage in their education, but action songs are the earlier version of musical instruments. The body is the first musical instrument.

A small group sing an action song in the room, and children join in as they arrive. Instead of waiting for all the children to arrive, which will waste time and be boring for the children who are sitting, waiting for things to start, the practitioner starts the on-the-spot action song, and then children simply join in as they tune in to this familiar song. This makes the whole thing a community session – relaxed, enjoyable, stimulating – and there is no need to nag children to sit nicely while they wait!

As children sing they need to give the movements of the song at the same time. Their body will accompany their singing.

So that children can manage in the early stages of an action song, practitioners will often ask them to sit in a circle around someone (for example, in the action song 'A Princess Lived in a High Tower' this would be the 'princess') and to do the actions with their upper bodies. Later on, as they become able to do the actions while singing the words, the children can move around in a circle as they sing and do the actions. But this requires them not only to control and manage their own body, as they sing and look, but also to be aware of where they are moving in relation to others in a circle dance. It will help if children have had plenty of previous experience with non-locomotion action songs. However, the biological maturation of the body also comes into this. Children aged from four to seven years will be at the point where this is an important part of their developing learning.

When children sing an action song it means that, in their heads, they have to pitch notes just ahead of each of the sounds they will sing or chant. Sally Goddard-Blythe (2004: 87) says this means children have to:

- visualize the sound in their mind
- anticipate their use of the internal ear
- motor plan where their actions will be
- respond to other people's singing and action, moving alongside them in the group
- combine all of this so that sensory motor skills integrate with feedback continuously going back to the ear and eye.

All of this will be invaluable in giving children key ways to make the journey into sensitive communication with others, talking and listening with engagement and focus, and reading and writing later on.

Phonological awareness

Children need to become phonologically aware if they are to move to later reading without difficulty. Phonological awareness is a global term (Mallett, 2005). It means becoming aware of the similarities and differences in sounds in a language and their patterns, tones, tempo and beat, loudness, softness, the *source* of the sound as well as the sounds.

The children are integrating the sounds and the actions so that their ears and eyes are working together through movement. This will help them later in reading and writing, when the eye and ear need to work in a co-ordinated way. They will need to be sensitive to each other as they do this

Becoming phonologically aware helps children on their journey into literacy. It paves the way for them to become **phonemically aware**. Being phonemically aware is all about hearing and being able to recognize the different phonemes (sounds) in a word (Mallett, 2005: 243).

Phonemes are the smallest units of sound in a word

In the following chapters we shall look at how developing both broad phonological and more detailed phonemic awareness helps children to get the most out of learning with nursery rhymes, poetry cards and story or information books. All of this will be happening in a richly enabling learning environment, both indoors and outdoors, where relationships are positive and children are respected as unique individuals.

Rhythm

A simple action song helps us to see how a child is developing understanding and confidence in the art of pattern-making. Songs and their accompanying actions provide opportunities for children to learn to express themselves with confidence, either socially in a group or alone at home with their families.

Singing action songs with children is enormous fun, but it is much more than that. It helps the brain to process some of the things that will be of key importance in developing the ability to talk and listen, develop good language and vocabulary, and to read and write. Developing a sense of rhythm is part of this.

Sally Goddard-Blythe (2004: 68) points out that both rhythm and sound are created as a result of movement. She says that:

- rhythm is a sequence of movements in time
- sound is made from vibrations.

Moving while they sing is therefore very important for young children, and especially for children with special needs and disabilities. Professor Adam Ockelford – a musician, educator and academic working with children with visual impairment and complex needs – has found that singing with actions is helpful. We can use the action song below to show this:

> Roly poly, roly poly, up, up, up,
> Roly poly, roly poly, down, down, down,
> Roly poly, roly poly give a little clap,
> Roly poly, roly poly, sit like that.

Children experience the words 'up', 'down' and 'clap' through movement. This is done in a sequence of sounds arranged in a pattern, which is called a **rhythm**.

The regular metred pattern is called the beat. Ros Bayley has developed the sense of **beat** in a rhythm through her songs for a puppet called 'Beat Baby'. Here an object is used to create a rhythmic accompaniment to a rhyme. Action songs create movements to accompany the words of a rhyme or song. In this case the arms go up along with the beat of the words, and a little higher each time the word 'up' is said. Both aspects are important, but it is the feedback, through making movements while singing, that gives powerfully integrated messages to the brain.

Rhyme

Children have a strong sense of rhyme, if encouraged to keep and develop this. With all brain functions it is a case of 'use it or lose it'. Some cultures place more emphasis on rhyme than others in the way music and dance, poetry and song are part of life for everyone.

Action songs are an introduction to rhyme. They are not about how a rhyme is written down. It is important to realize this, because there are many words in the English language which sound similar and rhyme, but will look quite different when written down.

Rhyme supports phonemic awareness

English is one of the most irregular, difficult languages in the world. Usha Goswami (2005; 2006; 2007) has researched this in some detail. She suggests that it is at its most irregular with the smallest units of sound (phonemes), but much more regular with the larger units of rhyming chunks of sound. This links with the cross-cultural research of Uta Frith and colleagues, which we explored in Chapter 5 on writing.

Morag Stuart (2006) suggested in a lecture that we need to know as much as we can about the contribution phonic knowledge makes to a child's development on the journey into literacy, proposing that many of the words children find in books are regular. However, Dominic Wyse and Morag Styles (2006: 21) argue that an emphasis on synthetic phonics is wrong, and that a more balanced approach to reading needs to prevail. Sue Ellis (in Goouch and Lambirth, 2007: 41) supports this, pointing out that most teachers are not 'exercised about the analytic/synthetic debate; good teachers respond to the patterns and possibilities children notice, and in practice the distinction is rarely as clear cut as theorists would believe'.

Rhyme engages a child's attention

There could be some agreement here between the different points of view. It is not just a question of the frequency with which children come across words and rhyming chunks. It is also about the meaning and pleasure given by rhyme. The brain has a propensity for patterns. Rhymes engage children (and adults) and we know that singing helps this process along.

Children need rhyming chunks to support the development of letter–sound correspondences and the processes of blending and segmenting. They make it easier for children to enjoy and engage with texts later on. They also provide powerful tools for children to focus, listen, look, move and integrate these in ways that support reading and writing.

This is why it is important to give children rich language environments both indoors and outdoors, with real and multi-sensory experiences.

The challenge for those of us who are working with young children is how to make it as easy as possible for them to communicate using the English language, and to help them on their journey into reading and writing so that they are not just reluctant and dutiful readers and writers, but also avid and enthusiastic bookworms and writers.

Hearing the patterns of the rhymes

The beauty of action songs is that they are not presented to children in a written-down form. Instead we will 'act' them out with children. They contain rhymes, with words that have similar sound patterns and rhythms. For example 'roly' sounds very similar to 'poly' in the action song. Children learn to hear the sameness in

The children sing while they do the actions. It helps them to sit on the floor to do this, so that they can use the upper body without having to co-ordinate it with the lower body. The brain develops from head to toe, so co-ordinating the legs with the rest of the body is hard to do

these words. They also begin to distinguish between the 'R' of Roly and the 'P' of Poly. This will be very important for learning to read print later on. They will become phonemically aware of the smallest sounds in the language.

When singing action songs, because they are not written down when presented to the children, the focus is on the patterns of sound which make the rhymes. There is no text to look at, so it not an issue that there are many words which rhyme when spoken but look different when written down. This means that some of the words in the songs sound the same, but are not spelt the same. Because the emphasis is on how the words sound in an action song, this does not matter.

In the photograph (page 107) you can see the children singing the action song, 'Wind the Bobbin Up'. The boys and the girls are engaged and focussed as they sing and do the actions. The adults in the pre-school playgroup have spaced themselves out so the children can watch and imitate an adult from wherever they are sitting.

Wind the bobbin up

Wind the bobbin up
Wind the bobbin up
Pull, pull, clap, clap, clap.

Point to the ceiling
Point to the floor
Point to the ceiling
Point to the floor.

Clap your hands together
One, two, three
Put your hands upon your knee.

Children need to be encouraged to concentrate at their own pace

The children are pointing to the ceiling as they sing the action song. The adult is looking at the end of her finger as she sings, and is exaggerating this movement so as to encourage it. Two girls are doing this. Other children are doing the action without tracking it with their eyes. One girl is slower to raise her arm, but is very focussed and engaged. Several children are singing but not doing the actions.

We need to remember, as Sally Goddard-Blythe demonstrates, that it is very challenging for children to co-ordinate the actions and the singing. They need plenty of repetition on different days in order to do this. Some children in the group are very young, just having turned three years old. They should not be rushed or nagged.

This is why it is a good idea to have **small groups** of children, so that adults can go at the right pace for the children singing the song. This gives those children who are just beginning to take part in action-song singing the time necessary to get the movements co-ordinated with the singing. It is easier to get this right with a small group. When practitioners work with large groups, inevitably some children will 'get lost', and there is a tendency to treat children as a herd to be driven along!

Extending the gaze

At first, babies gaze at faces, and will enjoy being talked to and sung to at this close distance.

The extended gaze goes from:

- face to face
- face to hands
- face to end of arms
- face to end of toes.

Seeing things at a more distant focus is important for reading print later on. Action songs are helpful in this. Babies watch their arms go up or down, and then they focus on the hand.

Action songs using the body, but on the spot (non-locomotion)

There are many action songs of this type. In the first stage they are sung while sitting on the floor (so that the child is grounded and not having to balance on a chair). The position is upright. The arms and hands and fingers of the upper body are the main focus. It is challenging for children to sing and do the actions at

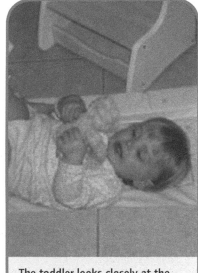

The toddler looks closely at the teddy bear and holds it up. Later, the gaze both near and far will be further developed through action songs

the same time. Adults often offer songs where the movements are too difficult to do at the same time as singing. If you consistently find yourself singing a solo, think again! Is this matching the child's development? It is important to sing the song and do the actions together and not separate the two, because co-ordinating these is of central importance. Imagine dancing without music! But it is also important to repeat the song quite a few times so that children stand a chance of learning the action song with you. It needs to be sung slowly enough for them to grasp the words and the movements.

Stage 1 action songs – upper body, simple rhymes and movements

We looked at 'Wind the Bobbin Up' (opposite). Froebel divided action songs into different types. This one is about objects. It is rather old fashioned today, in that children will not see a bobbin being wound up on a wool spinning wheel in the main. But it remains a much-loved song, and it could be used to introduce history and how wool was spun in previous times. Children who have been taken to a museum, and seen an adult do this with wool on a spinning wheel, will have better understanding of the words of the song. They will also appreciate history more easily if it is brought to life. 'Wind the Bobbin Up' is a Stage 1 action song and you will find some more below. They include songs from nature, and about objects and people, in the Froebelian tradition.

As always an action song such as 'Five Little Ducks' means more if real ducks have been experienced. Children bring meaning to songs if they have had meaningful experiences that relate to them. The richer a child's experience, the more they will understand and appreciate literature which deepens their thinking, feelings and relationships

Incy Wincy spider (animal type)

Incy Wincy spider
Climbed up the spout. (*Use the fingers of both hands to represent the spider climbing the spout*)

Down came the rain
And washed the spider out. (*Raise the hands and lower them slowly, wriggling fingers to be the rain*)

Out came the sunshine
Dried up all the rain. (*Raise the hands above the head together and spread them out and then down again*)

And Incy Wincy spider
Climbed the spout again. (*The same as the first lines*)

As children become more experienced with upper body, non-locomotion action songs, the actions can become more complex.

Stage 2 action songs – more upper body movement sequences and several verses

These are still:
- on the spot
- non-locomotion
- involving the upright position.

However, the movements involve:

- more complex sequences to remember
- several verses to sing.

In the baby song 'Round and Round the Garden' (see the photograph on page 59), the parent performs the actions for the child. When the child does their own actions, this shows a progression.

Little cottage in the wood

(*Make roof with hands*)

Little girl at the window stood
(*Look through holes when a circle is made out of the thumb and forefinger*)

Saw a rabbit running by
(Pound on the floor with feet)

Knocking at the door
(Knock one fist on the palm of the other hand)

'Help me, help me,' the rabbit cried
(Hands up and down in the air)

'Or the hunter will shoot me dead.'
(Pretend to aim and shoot)

'Little rabbit come inside
(Beckon with forefinger)

You'll be safe with me.'
(Hold the rabbit like a baby in folded arms)

The story element helps children to remember the narrative which is important for later reading. The actions, such as the feedback to the brain of the fist on the palm of the hand, are also important for later writing.

Stage 3 – whole-body non-locomotion action songs

The selection of action songs using the whole body has been carefully made to illustrate the range. Different movements involving the co-ordination of the upper and lower body are used.

Keeping the midline

We all clap hands together

We all clap hands together
We all clap hands together
Because it's fun to do

We all stand up together
We all sit down together
We all stamp feet together
We all turn round together

Bending from the middle – the vestibular system

These action songs link to the vestibular system in the body. They involve the tilting and tipping which Penny Greenland (2010) emphasizes as so important.

The children sit on the floor, and bend forwards and backwards as if they were rowing. Older children will sometimes like to sit one behind the other to do this, giving the impression of all being in a rowing boat and rowing together. However, co-ordinating your movements with someone else, even if they are doing the same thing, is quite a challenge. It might prove a challenge too far for very young children! Encouraging them to control their own movements is the thing to concentrate on at this stage.

Row, row, row your boat

Row, row, row your boat
Gently down the stream
Merrily, merrily , merrily , merrily
Life is but a dream.

Row, row, row your boat
Gently out to sea
Merrily, merrily, merrily, merrily
We'll be home for tea.

Row, row, row your boat
Gently on the tide
Merrily, merrily, merrily, merrily
To the other side.

Row, row, row your boat
Gently back to shore
Merrily, merrily, merrily, merrily
Home for tea at four.

Bending from the midline to the side

The child holds his or her arm in a curve down one side, and holds the arm out on the other side. This is quite a challenge for young children, because they have to do something different with each arm. They also have to tilt to 'pour', so that the out-held arm points towards the floor.

I'm a little teapot

I'm a little teapot
Short and stout
Here's my handle
Here's my spout.
When I see the tea cups
Hear me shout!
'Pick me up and pour me out.'

Sequences from top to toe

In this song, the same movement action works its way down from the head to the toes. Children are still on the spot but the movement is in a sequence. It is simple in that the same movement is performed each time. The two hands are placed flat on the head, shoulders, and so on. The child also has to turn on the spot, which can be quite a challenge at first.

Head and shoulders, knees and toes

Head and shoulders
Knees and toes, knees and toes.
Heads and shoulders, knees and toes.
We all turn round together.

This time, the movement is different in each verse, but still involves both sides of the body (hands together, feet doing the same movement, hands doing the same movement, and so on).

If you're happy and you know it

If you're happy and you know it
Clap your hands.
If you're happy and you know it
Clap your hands.
If you're happy and you know it
And you really want to show it
If you're happy and you know it
Clap your hands.
If you're happy and you know it
Stamp your feet (...and so on).

If you're happy and you know it
Tap your knees ...

Co-ordinating movements, singing the words and using a different pitch: a loud, soft and normal speaking voice

The actions are relatively simple here, but children will need to co-ordinate these with shouting loudly, or whispering softly, and with a normal pitch. Young children do find whispering difficult, and this song helps them to make the sound contrasts.

The movements involve shaking the head, wrists and feet, in a particular order. There is the glimmer of a story developing here. Children can anticipate the movements as the narrative unfolds through the character of the scarecrow.

I'm a dingle dangle scarecrow

When all the cows were sleeping and the sun had gone to bed,
Up jumped the scarecrow, and this is what he said:
'I'm a dingle-dangle scarecrow with a flippy, floppy hat.
I can shake my hands like this, and shake my feet like that.'

When all the hens were roosting, and the moon behind a cloud,
Up jumped the scarecrow, and shouted very loud:
'I'm a dingle-dangle ...' (*and so on*).

When the dogs were in the kennel, and the doves were in the loft,
Up jumped the scarecrow, and whispered very soft:
'I'm a dingle, dangle scarecrow ... (*and so on*).

IN SUMMARY

Action songs are a powerful way to support the development of the essentials of literacy.

- In Stages 1 and 2, they challenge children in their co-ordination of the arms and upper body. Movements and verses and narratives become increasingly complex.
- In Stage 3, the upper and lower body is used, but on the spot.
- Action songs support the integration of sound, sight and movement.
- They give a gentle introduction to narrative and the development of characters.
- They also give a gentle introduction to singing games.
- They help children with phonological awareness, through alliteration, rhyme and rhythm.

Key Terms

Personal tempo – this is the speed and pace at which the child prefers the music to move. A child will move most easily if the music suits their personal tempo

Phonemic awareness – this is becoming aware of and being able to identify and use the smallest sounds in the language

Phonological awareness – this is becoming aware of the sounds of the language and being able to hear and manipulate the way they fall into syllables and rhyming chunks

Pitch – this is about whether the music is high or low

Rhythm – this is the way that the sequence of sounds moves in time. It might have a steady beat, and this is very important for children to establish

Reading

Bayley, R. and Broadbent, L. (2004) *Helping Young Children with Steady Beat*. Birmingham: Lawrence Educational.
Ockelford, A. (1996) *All Join In: A Framework for making Music with Children and Young People who are Visually Impaired and have Learning Difficulties*. Peterborough: RNIB.

Further Reading

Bruce, T. (forthcoming) *Early Childhood Education* (4th edn). London: Hodder/Arnold.

Chapter 7

Action Songs – Moving Around

In this chapter we show how:

- action songs can be used for moving around;
- action songs can integrate body movement with sight and sound.

Why locomotion action songs come later

At first, children flail about when performing action songs involving moving around (locomotion). This is because they find it quite difficult to co-ordinate their feet and legs with their arms, hands and heads. It is even more difficult to do all of that and move about in a circle!

The chaotic scene of toddlers being required to perform 'Ring a Ring o' Roses' and falling over with wild abandon is a frequent occurrence. It is simply too difficult for a new walker to manage. It is not going to do any damage, and it can be great fun, but it does mean that the children are not yet ready to co-ordinate a steady beat with both their upper and lower halves.

Honing emerging skills

It is good for older children to be with younger children, so that the latter can see the possibilities and what lies ahead. They are eager to be with older children, providing they are not pressured to perform in advance of their competencies.

Older children also benefit from thinking of others who are less able to do what they can do, and helping them. But it is also important that children who are ready to hold a steady beat in locomotion action songs have the opportunity to do this. They need to hone their skills without becoming frustrated and giving up because of always being with younger children. Again, children need both. This is why small-group times are of central importance in getting things right for each unique child.

Co-ordinating movements with other people

Making and dancing in a circle is not an easy thing for very young children to do. It is best to do this in a small group. If children cannot manage this (and two- and three-year-olds will be challenged to do so) and if trying to make them do this becomes a nagging session, such that the group never gets to sing the song, then we should abandon it. There are other ways to sing an action song, as we saw in the previous chapter, and the new movements can be returned to when the children have more experience and biological maturation. Children need to be experienced, having sung action songs based on their upper body, or on the spot with the whole body (as we explored in the previous chapter), and able to develop sensitivity to moving in relation to each other.

It is more important for children to manage, control and co-ordinate their upper and lower body movements, without having to move with other people in mind. Once they can manage the movements while singing or chanting, they will often enjoy joining in with others in a dance-like way. Formation dances are early forms of dance, and we can see the glimmerings of this in the photograph of the children's spontaneous play.

Girls often take the lead in this, but boys will usually be watching them and thoroughly enjoying their performance. Children often spend time observing others before they decide to join in. Practitioners often report that boys often seem to wait and observe in this way more than girls when it comes to singing, dancing, drawing, mark-making and looking at books. But in other areas of development and learning they will make the first move, such as in working out mechanical problems and challenges, or with three-dimensional constructions such as wooden blockplay.

An emergent partner dance is developing here. Action songs give children ideas, and they will then choreograph their own versions of dances. This dance seems to have been inspired by the actions of the song showing how to cut a way through thick forest in a song about a princess in a high tower

Action songs involving locomotion

Travelling action songs

I went to school one morning, and I walked like this

> I went to school one morning, and I walked like this
> Walked like this, walked like this.
> I went to school one morning and I walked like this
> All on my way to school.
>
> I saw a little robin and he hopped like this . . . (and so on).
> I saw a shiny river and I splashed like this . . . (and so on).
> I saw a little pony and he galloped like this . . . (and so on).
> I saw a tall policeman and he stood like this . . . (and so on).
>
> I heard the school bell ringing and I ran like this . . . (and so on).

Jumping action songs

Three little monkeys jumping on the bed

> Three little monkeys jumping on the bed.
> One fell off and bumped his head.
> Mummy called the doctor
> And the doctor said:
> 'No more monkeys jumping on the bed!'
>
> Two little monkeys jumping on the bed.
> One fell off and bumped his head.
> Mummy called the doctor
> And the doctor said:
> 'No more monkeys jumping on the bed!'
>
> One little monkey jumping on the bed.
> He fell off and bumped his head.
> Mummy called the doctor
> And the doctor said:
> 'No more monkeys jumping on the bed!'

Here the actions are the same in each verse, but not all the children need to take part as only the monkeys must do the jumping. It is best if all the children have a turn at jumping, and so this action song is best with about six children.

Rolling action songs

It is easier to rotate the body by rolling on the floor than it is to turn around when standing up.

There were ten in the bed

There were ten in the bed
And the little one said,
'Roll over! Roll over!'
So they all rolled over
And one fell out.
He gave a little scream 'OW!'
He gave a little shout 'HEY!'
'That was very mean!'

There were nine in the bed . . . (and so on).

This song introduces 'voice sounds' and the hint of a story.

Crossing the midline by pointing

Did you ever see a lassie

Did you ever see a lassie
A lassie, a lassie,
Did you ever see a lassie
Go this way and that?

Go this way and that way,
Go this way and that way,
Did you ever see a lassie
Go this way and that?

Children can sit on the floor, in a circle, and with their hand above their eyebrow, as if saluting, turn their head in either direction, or they can point one way and then the other.

Later on they can do this as they move round in a circle, with one child placed in the centre as the lassie or the laddie.

Alternate sides

Here we go Looby loo

Here we go Looby loo,
Here we go Looby light,
Here we go Looby loo,
All on a Saturday night.

You put your left arm in,
You put your left arm out,
You shake it a little, a little,
And turn yourself about.

The next verses are:

> You put your right arm in . . . and so on.
> You put your left leg in . . . and so on
> You put your right leg in . . . (*and so on*)
> You put your whole self in . . . and so on

Early circle action songs

There are some action songs ('Looby Loo', 'Did You Ever See a Lassie') which make a good transition from children needing to be in one place and able to focus on their own body doing the actions while singing.

Children can sing this on the spot, or they can move round in a circle singing, for the chorus, and then stop to do the action. This helps them to manage the movements without having to worry about getting round in a circle, and being sensitive to what others are doing and where they are placed in the circle.

Here we go round the mulberry bush

> Here we go round the mulberry bush,
> The mulberry bush, the mulberry bush,
> Here we go round the mulberry bush,
> On a cold and frosty morning.

Children walk round in a circle, singing the chorus above. Then they stand still, and focus on doing the actions with their upper body only, as they sing:

> This is the way we wash our hands,
> Wash our hands, wash our hands,
> This is the way we wash our hands,
> On a cold and frosty morning.

They repeat the circle movements singing the chorus again, and then stop to sing the next more focussed movements as they sing.

> This is the way we wash our face . . .
>
> This is the way we comb our hair . . .
>
> This is the way we tie our shoes . . .

In this way the circle game is manageable for young children.

A much loved, but later locomotion song is the 'Hokey Cokey'. It involves standing still to do the more focussed actions, with running forward and backwards, or walking in a circle holding hands in between. It is more difficult to go forwards and backwards like this than the simpler walking round in a circle holding hands in the 'Mulberry Bush' earlier form of locomotion action song.

Hokey cokey

(Children hold hands in a circle and walk round singing)

> Oh, do the hokey, cokey.
> Oh, do the hokey, cokey.
> Oh, do the hokey, cokey,
> Knees bend, arms stretch,
> Ra, ra, ra.

Then they stand on the spot and do the actions:

> You put your left arm in,
> You put your left arm out,
> In, out, in out and shake it all about.
> You do the hokey cokey and you turn around,
> And that's what it's all about.

Then chorus again, with joined hands, run into the middle and retreat backwards, still holding hands. Release hands and do the actions with knees bent, and so on.
The next verses are:

> You put your right arm in . . .
> You put your left leg in . . .
> You put your right leg in . . .
> You put your whole self in . . .

Action songs that become ring games

Ring games involve children in rules which have an element of choice (Kalliala, 2005). An early and simple form is 'Sandy Girl'.

Sandy girl

> There's a little sandy girl
> Sitting on a stone
> Crying, crying, because she's all alone.
> Stand up, sandy girl
> Dry your tears away
> Chose one to be your friend
> And come out to play.

A boy or girl (or both) can be sandy people sitting in the centre of the circle with their hands over their eyes. The children walk round in a circle singing. Sandy people choose a child each to hold with both hands. They then turn round together on the spot, holding hands. The chosen children then go into the centre to become the sandy people.

A later, more complex form of ring game is 'In and Out the Dusty Bluebells'.

In and out the dusty bluebells

In and out the dusty bluebells
In and out the dusty bluebells
In and out the dusty bluebells
You shall be my partner.

Tippy, tappy, tippy, tappy on my shoulder,
Tippy, tappy, tippy, tappy on my shoulder,
Tippy, tappy, tippy, tappy on my shoulder,
You shall be my partner.

The children form a circle, and join hands to make arches.

One child runs in and out of the arches, and stops behind one of the children. The child touched comes out of the circle and, holding the shoulder of the one who chose them, follows in and out of the arches. All the children make a line in the end. This is a ring game. It involves children and choices in relation to the rules of the game. It also has elements of a formation dance, like those found in folk dances.

Ring games involving running

I sent a letter to my friend

I sent a letter to my friend
And on the way I dropped it.
One of you has picked it up
And put it in your pocket.
It wasn't you, it wasn't you
. . . It was you!

Children sing as they walk round in a circle, and then sit on the floor at the end of the verse. One has a piece of paper to represent the letter. This child walks round the outside of the circle, saying 'It wasn't you ...' and then drops it behind one of the children. This child jumps up and runs after the child who dropped the letter, trying to race them back to the empty space and sit in it. The child left without a space to sit in picks up the letter and the song begins again.

This song, because it is more complex (as is 'Dusty Bluebells'), is suitable for children when they are about six or seven years old.

Action songs that create a drama

An action song that tells a story is 'A Princess Lived in a High Tower'.

The photographs tell the story. Every culture seems to have different versions around this literary theme. In fact, all the finger rhymes and action songs in the book are cross-cultural in their themes. There are similar rhymes and songs everywhere in the world. The different languages of the world have their own rhythms, rhymes and sounds. Through these, children learn their culture, their language and are helped in their journey towards literacy. In this book we are thinking about how the particular action songs selected help and support children to learn the tones and feel of the English language. However, it is also invaluable to teach children action songs in different languages, so that their experience goes beyond English alone.

Stories like 'Rapunzel' and 'Sleeping Beauty' are more complex forms of this action song. These themes of literature are cross-cultural. The action song introduces the theme in a very engaging, easy-to-understand way. It is as if it gives the headlines for the more sophisticated version.

Verse 1

The princess stands in the centre of the ring of children:

> There was a princess long ago, long ago,
> Long ago.
> There was a princess long ago, long ago.

'There was a princess long, long ago'. In a previous chapter there was discussion of the way that dressing-up clothes can suggest a character for a child, and help them to take part in a narrative or, as in this case, an action song that tells a story. However, it is also important to act out songs without props. Variety is the key. In this way children are offered ideas, but they are also encouraged to use their imaginations, or to find materials to make their own costumes. It is never necessary to buy expensive outfits. The costume here is made from an old bedspread and a cardboard crown

Verse 2

The children raise their hands to make a tower:

> And she lived in a big high tower,
> A big high tower, a big high tower.
> And she lived in a big high tower,
> Long ago.

Verse 3

One child, as the fairy, waves her arm over the princess:

> One day a fairy waved her wand, waved her wand,
> Waved her wand.
> One day a fairy waved her wand, waved her wand.

Verse 4

The princess lies down and closes her eyes:

> The princess slept for a hundred years, a hundred years,
> A hundred years.
> The princess slept for a hundred years,
> A hundred years.

Verse 5

The children now wave their arms like trees:

> A great big forest grew around, grew around,
> Grew around.
> A great big forest grew around, grew around.

Verse 6

One child, as the prince, gallops round the outside of the ring:

> A gallant prince came riding by, riding by,
> Riding by.
> A gallant prince came riding by,
> Riding by.

'She lived in a big high tower'

Verse 7

He pretends to cut down the trees:

> He cut the trees down with his sword, with his sword,
> With his sword.
> He cut the trees down with his sword,
> With his sword.

Verse 8

He then wakes up the princess:

> He took her hand to wake her up, wake her up,
> Wake her up.
> He took her hand to wake her up,
> Wake her up.

'A great big forest grew around'

Verse 9

Children skip round clapping their hands:

> So everyone is happy now, happy now, happy now.
> So everyone is happy now, happy now.

Using play props to revisit the song

In the next chapter, we look at the importance of nursery rhymes and the use of dressing-up clothes and props in helping children on their journey into traditional English literature and literacy.

'He cut the trees down with his sword'

'He took her hand to wake her up'

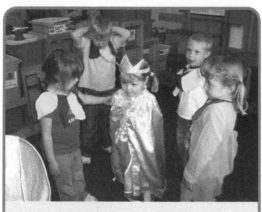

'Everyone is happy now'

These help children to hear the sounds of the English language. Throughout this book it is important to note that these are located within the richness of an enabling learning environment, that will include songs, music and dance from diverse cultures.

In the photographs of the princess in her tower, you can see how the children have raided the dressing-up box and found appropriate clothes for the characters. It is important that children have opportunities to revisit action songs, nursery rhymes and other songs in their own time and in their own way. Not all children come alive when they are in an adult-led group. They may appreciate trying out the songs in a more private context, quietly with a few friends, or alone. A carefully selected dressing-up area is therefore important (see Chapter 2).

Is it worth continuing the tradition of singing action songs with children?

This is a very easy question to answer. In a word – yes.

IN SUMMARY

Action songs are a sound tradition that is worth keeping because they:

- support important developmental processes in the brain, which will be useful and crucial in the journey through communication, language and literacy
- give children powerful ways of engaging with, understanding and participating in cultural events such as community singing and dancing
- contain cross-cultural literary themes which are found throughout the world
- help children to work out what it is to be a symbol user and sing other people's songs and actions (being a performer), and develop ideas about being a symbol maker, so they can create their own action songs
- act as a bridge from finger rhymes and fine motor control, to story and drama on a larger scale
- give children manageable experiences of rhythm and steady beat in movement and song

- encourage children to remember, imitate and be imitated
- support the integration of on-the-spot and locomotive movement, sight and sound, in the English language
- help children to be co-ordinated in their upper and lower bodies, so that, quite literally, they are whole people
- encourage children to create their own action songs
- give children the essentials for later literacy.

Key Terms

Choreographing a dance – a dance that is not spontaneous but planned so it may be repeated at different times

Literary themes – there seem to be universal themes in stories and songs which can be found in every culture, such as good overcoming evil, finding and loss

Reading

Opie, I. and Opie, P. (1988) *The Singing Game*. Oxford and New York: Oxford University Press.

Further Reading

Liebschner, J. (1992) *A Child's Work: Freedom and Guidance in Froebel's Educational Theory and Practice*. Cambridge: Lutterworth.

Chapter 8

Nursery Rhymes

In this chapter we show how:

- to help children learn nursery rhymes;
- to get to know the songs using props and acting;
- rhymes can support phonological awareness;
- rhymes can cover a range of literature and support beginning readers;
- rhymes can help develop vocabulary.

Children have a natural sense of drama. They enjoy the rhymes and miniature stories they tell. They also delight in the characters and situations. Nursery rhymes support the development of phonological and phonemic awareness. Children benefit from a sensitive introduction to a core of carefully selected nursery rhymes which can be used to foreground the natural engagement of children (and adults!) with rhythm, rhyme, alliteration and initial sounds. A small core of nursery rhymes should be selected and put to specific use. Alongside this there will be a wider range of much loved rhymes which, in a less focussed way, will cover a rich range of literature.

Children who are familiar with the traditional canon of nursery rhymes and some modern ones are at a great advantage in learning to read. They are learning about syllabification and rhyming chunks in a very enjoyable way. When these phonic strategies are taught in isolation it is much harder for children to grasp the concepts involved, and then there is a tendency to drill children. Over-teaching damages learning. For example, the initial sounds 'b' and 'sh', 'm', 'h', 'd', 'p' and 's', can be introduced and highlighted through the nursery rhymes, 'Mary, Mary Quite Contrary,' 'Humpty Dumpty' and 'See Saw, Margery Daw'.

It is important to make sure that children understand the vocabulary and that the rhymes have meaning for them. In Chapter 2 there are examples of how this can be done in an enabling environment with positive relationships.

Nursery rhymes are part of the canon of literature in the English language

Nursery rhymes give children a **canon of literature** that connects them with the traditions of their culture. Every culture has its own equivalent of nursery rhymes. It is important that children are introduced to a wide range of nursery rhymes, tapping into their diversity and richness across the world: 'It is likely that sensitivity to the rhythms and sound patterns of language is a universal feature of all cultures and their languages, as songs, poems, dances and music from around the world all indicate' (Whitehead, 2009: 23).

The sounds of language

Children who grow up speaking and hearing different languages, and who become bilingual and multilingual, are at a great advantage. They are able to pick up on the **phonology** (sound patterns) of different languages with more sensitivity than children who are monolingual. However it is natural for all children, and indeed adults, to be drawn to rhythm, rhyme and alliteration.

In earlier chapters we have seen that the brain is hardwired for the sounds of languages. But unless children are introduced to rhymes from birth, they are likely to lose, rather than further develop, the range of possibilities for hearing the sounds of:

- alliteration (which uses the same or similar sounds at the beginning of words)
- rhyme (which takes the ear to the sounds at the ends of words)
- rhythm (which is about syllabification – the part of a word pronounced as one beat)
- steady beat (this aspect of rhythm, is explored in the chapters on action songs)
- phonological awareness (hearing differences and similarities in sounds, such as alliteration, rhyme and rhythms, builds up phonological awareness)
- phonemic awareness (being able to hear and recognize phonemes, which are the smallest unit of meaningful sound in a word, also builds up phonological awareness).

'The Grand Old Duke of York'. This is an example of a nursery rhyme with manageable chunks to remember. It has a steady marching beat, and actions that go up and down. There is also rhyming, but 'men' and 'again' do not look as if they rhyme. At this stage of singing and getting to know nursery rhymes there is no emphasis on the written text at all. The songs are sung and acted out, and pictures are shown alongside the text in books, with no pressure to focus on the printed words

Margaret Mallett (2005: 243) suggests that sensitivity to the phonemic structure of spoken words is linked with success in reading. Others in the field would agree (Bryant and Bradley, 1985; Goswami and Bryant, 1990; Clay, 1998; Stuart, 2006; Snowling and Hulme, 2007).

Building a memorable and meaningful vocabulary – nursery rhymes can help

Marian Whitehead (2009: 21) points out that alliteration, rhyme and rhythm help us to remember. In ordinary conversations it is difficult to recall exactly the words we say to each other. Rhymes make it easier to do so. Because of this they help children to remember new words and build their vocabulary. Children with narrow language and poor vocabularies have more difficulty in reading and writing. Nursery rhymes help to overcome this, as well as reaffirm and consolidate those children with wide vocabularies.

Introducing a few carefully selected nursery rhymes with which to develop phonemic awareness

In olden days, few children would have encountered books in their homes, but, children were introduced to nursery rhymes because these would have been sung to them. In this way, they developed sensitivity to the sounds which would become so important when they later began to engage with decoding and encoding as they learned to read and write.

Nowadays many children have the advantage of books from a few months of age. The New Labour government set up the 'Books for Babies' scheme which has been very successful, so that babies receive books before they walk, and as toddlers.

Experience shows that children benefit hugely by exposure to books from an early age. Right from the start, lots of opportunities should be provided for children to engage with books that fire their imagination and interest. They should be encouraged to choose and peruse books freely as well as sharing them when read by an adult.

Enjoying and sharing books leads to children seeing them as a source of pleasure and interest and motivates them to value reading. (DfES, Letters and Sounds, 2007b: 2)

This is where nursery rhymes are so helpful. Singing these, and using props so that children can connect with them in a three-dimensional way, helps children to develop focus so that they engage with the sounds and actions with the phonological awareness that is needed to read and write.

Children are helped when:

- baby songs are introduced in three stages (Chapter 3)
- finger rhymes are introduced in three stages (Chapter 4)
- action songs are introduced in three stages (Chapters 6 and 7)
- nursery rhymes are introduced in two stages (Chapter 8 and 9).

Mary, Mary quite contrary's garden. The childminder has made some play props. The following year she realized that she did not need to do this. The children had begun making their own play props, encouraged and supported by her

Nursery rhymes – Stage 1: phonemic awareness

This means helping children to hear and distinguish the smallest units of sounds in words. Listening to the words and sounds so that children distinguish between and recognize the alliterations, rhythms and rhymes helps this process along. The nursery rhyme is first introduced, sung and acted out, and props are used. The text is not emphasized at this stage. This does not mean that children should be deprived of the print form of the nursery rhyme, but it does mean that the sounds are the focus and not the print. This is the message in this chapter. It is important to choose a small core of nursery rhymes which highlight phonemic awareness. Others can be enjoyed in a more general way, rather than in the specific ways focussed on in this chapter.

'Bye Baby Bunting'. The children have sung the song with the practitioner in a small group, sitting under a tree in the garden. Then they collected the scrambling net, with the adult helping to carry it to a spot with soft ground. Children were then invited to be the baby, and the volunteers took turns to sing the song and act it out. It was very popular with the children, and without any pressure the song was repeated over and over again. By the end of the session the children really knew the nursery rhyme

The girl shows quiet pride in showing the model she has made of Humpty's wall. It is interesting that she has selected egg boxes to do this. She is bearing in mind that Humpty is an egg. The first time the children were introduced, they sang the song, and then it was repeated using a real egg with a face drawn on it. The egg was then scrambled and eaten. It would be important to check if any children have egg allergies before introducing this set of props for this nursery rhyme

Using nursery rhymes – strengthening what comes naturally to children

Do not pressure children to articulate sounds they are still biologically developing

It is important to bear in mind that some sounds are more difficult than others for children to make. This is a developmental matter. The following sounds – developed with the guidance of linguists, educators and speech and language experts – are taken from the trainers' booklet, *Communicating Matters* (DfES, 2005a) and from discussions with the speech and language therapist who worked in our team.

As teachers of children with hearing impairments and speech and language specialists know, some of the easiest sounds to hear and say in English are **p, b, m, n** (pronounced as in **pot, baby, Mum** and **no**).

The sounds **h, w, t, d, g, k, y** (pronounced as in **hallo, why?, tomorrow, Dad, Gran, kite, you**) are more difficult for children who are speaking English so that a listener who does not know them well cannot understand what the child is saying.

By five years old, most children will be able to blend sounds in English. This means that as they speak they will use the sounds **sh, ch, bl, fl, sl, sn, st, cr, gr, sm, str** (as pronounced in **shell, chat, blue, floor, slippery, snake, station, crane, growl, smile strange**). They can usually say the sound 'f'.

But many children entering Year 1 in Key Stage 1 will not yet easily say the sounds **l, z, v, s, r, th** (as pronounced in **lap, zoo, vet, sugar, rabbit, thumb**).

Children can hear phonemic/sound differences before they can say them

We worked with a speech and language therapist, who emphasized the importance of giving children nursery rhymes with a clear contrast in the phonemes (the smallest units of sound in a word). We found that nursery rhymes, with their phonograms (an initial sound followed by rhyming chunk) such as 'See Saw, Margery Daw', do this quite naturally. We also found that some nursery rhymes can be quite confusing. Perhaps this is behind the angry and passionate debates about rhyme in recent years. Not all rhymes are helpful. But if carefully selected, they can give huge and valuable support to children when developing the phonic aspects of reading and writing.

Issues of inclusion and diversity

The outline of the biological development of the sounds children articulate gives very general statements.

Some children have special needs, learning difficulties and disabilities. Others speak English as an additional language and, if they are new arrivals, the sounds of the English language may be new to them. Some children will have engaged in sensitive communication with adults from birth, with rich language development, able to interact and focus their attention in 'shared sustained conversations' (Siraj-Blatchford et al., 2002). Others have been given puréed food for most of their lives, so that they find chewing difficult and difficulty in forming many of the sounds of English (or any languages). They may also spend long periods of time in front-facing pushchairs, unable to see the faces of adults pushing them, and not being spoken to directly for much of the day, or able only to peep out with only a sideways view of the world, and no face-to-face contact in the type of pushchair that stacks children one above the other. Adults might also use mobile phones, so that talking is not interactive with the child. But every child in the first five years deserves our commitment and help in developing communication and language on their journey into literacy.

Humpty Dumpty falls over again, and the rhyme is chanted over and over again. The boys (typically) respond enthusiastically to this three dimensional play with the nursery rhyme

Is there an ideal order for helping children to distinguish and hear the sounds of the English language in a way that will help them towards reading and writing?

It makes sense to introduce the sounds that are important for reading and writing English in ways which help children to discriminate them most easily. Bearing this in mind, we found ourselves on a journey which proved to be fascinating. We wanted to try and link the biologically-driven understandings children have of the sounds of the English language with the recommended order of sounds in *Letters and Sounds* (DfES, 2007b) which suggests a completely different order. We were interested to find that some of the easier sounds to produce were suggested for introduction later, and some of the more difficult sounds were suggested for earlier inclusion.

However, this document – which is for guidance and has no legal requirement that it must be followed – very helpfully stresses: 'This is not a list to be worked through slavishly, but to be selected from as needed for an activity' (2007b: 48).

The boys began singing 'Mary, Mary Quite Contrary' while gardening. No-one told them to do this. It was their idea. This resonates with the time-honoured tradition of people working in the fields at harvest time or fruit-picking time, singing as they work. It seems to be a basic human response

Upholding the principles of the Early Years Foundation Stage

We developed a set of core nursery rhymes which would introduce children to some of the basic sounds, with a systematic approach in the phonological aspects of learning to read and write. This needed to be done in ways that support the first five years and continue that learning journey into statutory primary education.

Traditional nursery rhymes selected to develop phonemic awareness

Mary, Mary quite contrary

> Mary, Mary quite contrary,
> How does your garden grow?
> With silver bells,
> And cockle shells,
> And pretty maids all in a row.

Contrasting sounds

Children, as they sing and act out the rhyme, can soon be helped to hear the differences in:

- bells and shells.

Although there are other rhyming words, they are more difficult because of the way they are spaced apart in the rhyme. 'Grow' and 'row' are not as easy for the brain to sort out, so it is best to focus on 'bells' and 'shells' which contrast with each other more obviously. Using props (real bells and shells) makes it easier for children to note the 'b' that goes with 'bell' and the 'sh' sound that goes with 'shell'. This is a multi-sensory approach.

In these photographs, there are examples of children becoming involved in some of the sounds of 'Mary, Mary Quite Contrary'.

- 'b' in bell and 'sh' in shell.

This encourages children to listen to sounds at the beginning of words, and to hear the difference between the 'b' and the 'sh'.

It is important to talk about the sound at the **beginning of the word** (initial sounds).

- the words rhyme: b-ell and sh-ell.

This naturally also encourages children to listen to the **rhyme** that sounds the same. It is important to give children the word 'rhyme'.

We found that children responded easily when the sounds were very different at the beginning of the word, and made a good contrast ('b' and 'sh' fall into that category).

Children will also enjoy the **alliteration** (repetition) of 'm' in 'Mary, Mary'. Some might even take the word into their vocabulary. If not, it is important to explain that there are the same sounds at the beginning of 'Mary, Mary'.

Humpty Dumpty sat on a wall

Humpty Dumpty sat on a wall,
Humpty Dumpty had a great fall.
All the King's horses and all the King's men,
Couldn't put Humpty together again.

In this rhyme, children quickly hear the difference between the 'H' sound in Humpty and the 'D' sound in Dumpty. Once again, there is no emphasis on the written form at this point. Children are given books of nursery rhymes to enjoy, and the various props for singing and acting out the song. They are encouraged to hear the difference in the sounds of the two bits of Humpty Dumpty's name.

In this way, children begin to distinguish between 'm', 'b', 'sh', 'h' and 'd' in these rhymes. They do so through enjoyment of

Singing the familiar rhyme helps memory of similar sounds (rhyming chunks) and differences (initial word sounds)

Building Humpty Dumpty's wall

the two nursery rhymes, and the encouragement to focus on particular words in the rhymes as they listen to them.

Enjoying the singing and together acting out the nursery rhyme are the most important things

We are likely to put children off if we over-teach. Over-teaching (Langer, 1997) damages learning. The younger the child, the greater the damage that can be done. The aim is to support children's natural delight in rhyme, alliteration and rhythm, and to open up the world of literacy and literature in doing so. 'Pushing a child toward a new skill too soon can cut short the preceding period of organisation and preparation which provides the basis for later automaticisation of functioning' (Goddard-Blythe, 2004: 48).

Alliteration

Children will probably already know the rhyme 'Peter Pointer' by this time. They readily take to listening to the alliteration of the 'p' sound at the beginning of 'Peter' and 'Pointer'. In order that they may have another experience of alliteration, this time contrasting with the 'M' in 'Mary, Mary', this would be a good time to introduce another suitable rhyme.

Children can enjoy the alliteration of the 's' sound in 'See saw'. The rhyme makes a memorable backcloth which aids phonemic awareness through the alliteration of 's'.

See saw, Margery daw

See saw, Margery daw,
Johnny shall have a new master.
He shall have but a penny a day,
Because he can't work any faster.

The importance of not rushing children through their journey into literacy

Before introducing children to Stage 2 nursery rhymes through poetry cards (see the next chapter), it is important to ensure that children are not being rushed. After all, when a child becomes an adult and attends an interview for a job, no one is going to ask these questions of them:

- At what age were you toilet trained?
- When did you begin to sleep through the night as a baby?
- At what age did you begin to read and write?

Early is not important. Early is not best. What matters is that the child becomes a lifelong reader and writer, a bookworm, and someone who takes pleasure in literature and seeking information and reflecting on thoughts, feelings and relationships through reading and writing. It is not advisable to rush children through the important beginnings of their journey into literacy – they cannot continue to travel well if the essentials are not in place. The focus here has been on time-honoured essentials that have stood the test of time across the world.

It is always important not to throw out the baby with the bath water. New research findings, as yet not reliable, might indicate a greater emphasis on one aspect or another, depending on the interests of particular researchers, funders and politicians. There is currently a focus on phonic work, and this is narrowing into synthetic phonics. This is not based on robust research (Goswami, in Goouch and Lambirth, 2007; Wyse and Goswami, 2008), it is based on ideology. The most significant thing is, however, that phonics work – whether in the narrow use of synthetic phonics, or the broader use of three grain sizes (syllables, rhyming chunks and phonemes) – is deeply embedded within a broad and rich language environment, which enables development and learning both indoors and outdoors.

Before introducing poetry cards

Before introducing poetry cards (explored in the next chapter) we must be sure that children are confident and competent in all the aspects outlined below. These connect to the framework documents of the four countries of the UK.

Official documents come and go – some with longer life spans than others, and some with statutory force. The key aspect here is to identify the main messages in the documents and see how they match the core messages of early childhood practice in the four countries of the UK. Official documents should never dictate practice. That action leads to unthinking practice, which will be of poor quality. But they should support early childhood practice that is based on time-honoured principles and established through research and theory. They can then be used as a resource for reflective practice. The 'Aspects' which follow are reworded from a non-statutory document, *Letters and Sounds* (DfES, 2007b), in the kind of language that is resonant in this book.

Aspect 1 environmental sounds

- Are adults and children spontaneously playing and talking together?
- Are they exploring sounds that different animals, objects, languages, accents and dialects make, and the everyday sounds of life, such as traffic in the street?

'The Gingerbread Man' – rhythm and rhyme. The refrain in the story encourages rhythm and rhyme, 'Run, run as fast as you can, You can't catch me I'm the gingerbread man'

- Are the adults helping children to hear the sounds of different languages and to learn some of the different sounds, such as 'r' in French and 'th' in English or 'g' in Arabic?
- Are the adults encouraging language for thinking and feeling?
- Are they encouraging shoulder and other gross motor movements?
- Are they making role-play areas? And props for play scenarios?
- Are they going on listening walks with the children?
- Do they encourage quiet listening to sounds?
- Are children and adults exploring sounds outdoors and indoors?
- Are they using musical instruments and making them, too?
- Are they playing games with sounds in them?
- Are they making sure the groups are very small (eight is a large group, two to four will comprise a small group)?
- Are they using props with sounds in stories and rhymes (action songs and nursery rhymes and stories)?

Gradually children will start to identify what a sound is, and know where it comes from. They will also find similar sounds and develop language to describe the sounds. In this they will actively engage with other children.

Aspect 2 – instrumental sounds

Are you doing all of these things?

- Encouraging children to make musical instruments and to talk about the sounds they make?
- Using musical instruments indoors and outdoors?
- Observing which children make patterns of rhythm?
- Giving the opportunity for children to revisit adult-led experiences in their own way and choosing, and in their free-flow spontaneous play?
- Seeing if children listen to each other and respond as they play?

- Putting new words to old familiar songs sometimes?
- Giving children musical instruments when singing with them?
- Encouraging children to know and recognize which sounds different instruments make?
- Helping children to play loudly and softly, and to follow or lead in playing an instrument?
- Making sound effects when telling stories and rhymes?
- Encouraging children to 'play' instruments and listen to each other?

You will help the children to increase their vocabulary of sound descriptions, to match a sound to its source, to use sounds imaginatively in rhymes and stories, and to know which sounds they like and dislike.

Aspect 3 – body percussion

Is the following happening:

- Are children spontaneously splashing, stamping and making sounds in the garden with rhythm?
- Are adults encouraging rhythm and beat as they sing action songs, nursery rhymes and poetry cards?
- Are children enjoying the contrasts in speed and loudness?
- Are they joining in with the words and actions?
- Articulating the words easily?
- Keeping in time to the beat?
- Imitating the sounds and actions?
- Making up their own patterns of sound?

Making music – rhythm. Banging with the sticks as he sings 'Hickory dickory dock, The mouse ran up the clock', the rhythm goes right though this child's body

Children will begin to make up their own stories and rhymes, talk about the sounds they hear and group sounds (as loud and soft, fast and slow).

Aspect 4 – rhythm and rhyme

Is the following happening:

- Are you helping children to develop a stock of familiar rhymes and poems by hearing them over and over again?
- Are you helping children with disabilities and learning difficulties to access these in ways that are right for them as unique individuals?

Wiggly wiggly worms – alliteration helps children to become aware of the sounds at the beginnings of words

- Are you making sure that children with English as an additional language understand the poetry or rhyme, and are being helped to tune into the rhythm and sound of the English language?
- Are you sharing books with children?
- Are you encouraging children to give alternative words to familiar songs?
- Are you encouraging children to use the ideas from the rhymes, poetry and stories you tell them and read to them in the role-play area and with the story-box props, small world, and so on?
- Do you have books with rhymes in them?
- Do you sing finger rhymes, action songs and nursery rhymes every day?
- Do you point out initial sounds and rhymes in the songs?
- Do you play with words – for example, clapping the syllables in each child's name?

Gradually, children will see a pattern in the syllables of words, sing and chant rhyming strings, and recognize when words rhyme. They will join in with making a rhythmic sound, imitate rhythms they hear and keep to the beat. They will also make their own rhymes and rhythms.

Aspect 5 – alliteration

Is the following in place:

Voice sounds (yuk!) – a piece of mouldy apple. Voice sounds encourage children to create sound effects, and this makes them more conscious of the sounds they can make

- Children are enjoying saying things like 'wiggly worms', or when adults sing and read them rhymes?
- The book corner has rhymes with alliteration in them?
- Adults are pointing out initial sounds to children?
- Children are enjoying it when adults help them to think of and find words with the same starting sound – for example, when they sing and act the Humpty Dumpty nursery rhyme?
- Are adults careful not to exaggerate the sound at the beginning – 'p' not 'puh'?

Aspect 6 – voice sounds

Is the following happening:

- Do you encourage children to vocalize sounds and make up onomatopoeic ones ('Ouch!')?
- Children enjoying talking about the sound? ('Yum' when they enjoy eating something is a shorter sound than the long sound in 'Ooooooooooou!' when they have to swerve to avoid something on their bike.)
- Do you tell them rhymes with voice sounds in them?

Aspect 7 – oral blending and segmenting

Is the following in place:

- Do children engage with the nursery rhymes adults have introduced?
- Do they enjoy making a steady beat?
- Do they enjoy the rhyme aspect?
- Do they, with adult help, pick out the initial sound 'm' for 'Mary, Mary Quite Contrary'?

If a child is engaging with all seven aspects within the four principles of the *Early Years Foundation Stage* (a unique child; positive relationships; enabling environments outdoors and indoors; development and learning), then we can think about introducing poetry cards to children and their parents.

Poetry cards make a bridge for a child. They give children the next steps in their journey into literacy. They support phonic work with a meaningful introduction, which engages the interest and enjoyment of children until they are about seven years old. They keep children connected and anchored in the essentials of communication, language and literacy.

IN SUMMARY

In this chapter, we have:

- taken a specific focus. A few nursery rhymes have been carefully selected to introduce children to the sounds of the English language in ways that can specifically help children to develop syllabification, rhyming chunks, and phonemic awareness as three different grains of phonic work;
- continued the pattern throughout the book, by emphasizing that this needs to be located within the broad, rich and deep framework of good early childhood practice, with positive relationships, enabling environments for communication, language and literacy for each child;
- reminded ourselves that it is important to bring such rhymes alive for children before introducing them.

KEY TERMS

Alliteration – consecutive words begin with the same sound (wiggly wiggly worm)

Grains of phonic work – largest grain are syllables – don-key (two syllables); middle grain are rhyming chunks – scrunch, munch; smallest grain are phonemes (ch-a-t)

Syllable – the part of the word that is pronounced as one beat (love–ly), two syllables

Reading

Bruce, T., Meggitt, C. and Grenier, J. (2010) *Childcare and Education* (5th edn). London: Hodder Arnold.

Further Reading

Barrs, M. and Meek Spencer, M. (2007) 'Inquiry into meaning: a conversation', in K. Goouch, and A. Lambirth (eds), *Understanding Phonics and the Teaching of Reading: Critical Perspectives*. Maidenhead: Open University Press/McGraw-Hill Education.

Chapter 9

Poetry Cards: Mapping Sounds onto Letters

> In this chapter we show how:
>
> - syllables, rhyming chunks and phonemes work;
> - sounds map onto letters;
> - how poetry cards help children with inconsistencies in the sounds and written form of English;
> - how poetry cards can introduce children to traditional literature.

Why use poetry cards?

The introduction of poetry cards to children and parents emerges out of all the other experiences in the book, and should be seen as part of the broader context in engaging children in the essentials of literacy (see the audit of what needs to be in place at the end of the previous chapter).

Poetry cards help small groups (of about two to four children) in very enjoyable and engaging ways, towards becoming lifelong bookworms, avid writers and information seekers, creative artists and performers of dramas. Poetry cards are also a way of working which is in tune with the principles and approaches of the official framework documents of the four UK countries.

Poetry cards help children:

- to develop further into phonemic awareness
- to pick out letters, especially initial sounds and letters, and to recognize words and work out the patterns they naturally seek out and love to find

- with alliteration, rhythm, syllabification and rhyming chunks, to which they are more naturally drawn than phonemes
- with a steady rhythm, which is important for memorizing and word recognition
- with repetition, supporting memory, sight and sound co-ordination
- with simple rhymes involving a highlighted cvc (consonant, vowel, consonant) word
- with rhyming strings that are easily developed from key words
- with initial letters/sounds that are easily demonstrated in the key words emphasized
- through providing a rich and interesting text to read
- because the texts are in small and manageable chunks
- with mapping sounds onto letters (making the phoneme/grapheme connection)
- by giving them appropriate experiences with the alphabetic code, blending and segmenting, and reversing these
- by helping parents and practitioners to share and enjoy reading with them, thus supporting them as 'beginner' readers
- by helping their literacy experiences as they borrow poetry cards to take home to make meaning from small, manageable chunks of text
- by helping them to understand that print represents meaning
- by helping those with learning difficulties and disabilities to enjoy literature
- because they are multi-sensory and link holistically with all the areas of development and learning
- because they engage those who have English as an additional language to tune into English through small, manageable chunks of text, both rhythmic and musical
- by helping practitioners to develop their subject knowledge about literacy
- by creating a richly enabling language learning environment with multi-sensory experience in a meaningful context.

Poetry cards give an opportunity for children to engage in discussions about text and also about literature. A story about leaving porridge to stand for nine days is riveting and shocking as the smells and slime grow! Making pease porridge with the children, tasting it, chatting about it, and then leaving it for nine days is a major experience.

There were lively discussions in the group of practitioners on training days about whether it should be called pease pudding or pease porridge. For northerners there was no doubt it was pudding. The southerners among us insisted it was porridge.

What are poetry cards?

Poetry cards are made from carefully chosen, well-known, traditional nursery rhymes. They are first introduced through practical experiences (see Chapter 2) to ensure that children fully understand the vocabulary. A child needs to have made pease porridge/pudding, danced a jig, or visited a market before the poetry card is introduced.

We taught children who were ready to map sounds onto letters to use two poetry cards.

Making the poetry card

Writing out the poetry card

- The rhyme is written out on a large card (the bigger the better – think pantomime!).
- Make the print (in lower case) large, bold and clear.

Introduce the rhyme

- In a small group (eight is a large group; two to four children make a small group).
- In a quiet corner.
- By singing it daily all the way through ('Pease porridge hot').
- So that when it is familiar and well known it will be less challenging.

Pease porridge hot
Pease porridge cold
Pease porridge in the pot
9 days old.

Some like it hot
Some like it cold
Some like it in the pot
9 days old.

The aspects we selected

- **Alliterative** initial sounds 'p' in pease porridge.
- Same **initial sound** in second poetry card: 'pig'.
- Introduction to **rhyming strings:** 'pot', 'hot' and 'pig', 'jig'.
- Could be expanded to longer strings if children were ready.
- **Cvc words**, (pot, hot, pig, jig) suitable for blending, segmenting and reversing.
- Regular in both how the rhymes sounded and how they looked in print.

We wanted to introduce phoneme and grapheme links which involved some of the sounds of speech that children could most easily form. The sounds 'h' and 'p' come early, and are usually articulated in the speech of most three-years-olds.

Having said that, the speech and language therapist who worked with us stressed that hearing the difference between the sounds was the most important thing. It is therefore good to use contrasting sounds, such as 'h' and 'p'.

Why introduce one poetry card rather than another?

It is important to think carefully why a particular poetry card should be introduced. With the introduction of nursery rhymes, in the last chapter, the emphasis was on the sounds of alliteration, rhythm and rhyme. The emphasis is different with the introduction of poetry cards. The rhyming words emphasized must SOUND and LOOK the same (i.e. be spelt in the same way) if they are to be helpful.

> Doctor Foster
> Went to Gloucester
> In a shower of rain.
> He stepped in a puddle
> Right up to his middle
> And never went there again.

The sounds and look ('Doctor Foster', 'Gloucester') are not the same in this rhyme. This would not make a useful poetry card.

Using the poetry card 'Pease porridge hot'

- Children are naturally drawn to enjoying rhyming chunks. It is hard to stop them from finding these patterns in the words once they have been introduced to them, providing they are repeated often enough.

It is important for children to build an understanding that print represents the symbols which carry meaning, and can be read. It is also important that they approach print with a developing sensitivity to the way sounds are mapped onto it

- You will find yourself able to discuss alliteration (pease porridge). Children will be naturally drawn to alliteration, and once found they are fascinated and will delight in it.
- Rhyming strings are part of the essentials of literacy, and are a strong component of poetry cards (hot, pot, got, lot, dot, jot).
- Chukovsky (1963) and Opie and Opie (1988) were famous for their work in gathering examples of the joy children take in nonsense rhymes of their own making. Children need to know rhymes in order to make their own.

- Encourage the children to predict the next word, discuss why they are right, and how they came to that decision – 'because it rhymes ... because the sound is "p" and then "o"and then "t", so it says "pot"', and so on. In this way, children develop the language of literacy, that will help them to appreciate literature, too.

We emphasized 'hot' and 'pot'.

Using props to 'act out' the song and get to know the words

- These were the last words in the line.
- We were careful to articulate the sounds clearly for the children (as we had done in singing the oral and aural nursery rhymes – see Chapter 7): p-o-t (not puh-oh-tuh).
- We selected these words because they had three phonemes, with a single syllable, and they also rhyme.
- We segmented, and children joined in if they wished or were able to.
- Pick out the initial **grapheme** you have selected (for example, 'p' in 'pot'). Link this with children's names **of the same letter**.
- This should be at the end of the line.
- Give children the name of the sound it makes in this situation. It is important to say the sound correctly. (for example, 'p' or 'h' without putting an extra 'uh' sound on the end; e.g. 'P' as in 'Patrick', 'Parvel').
- Having introduced the **sounds** in the initial letters of words ('p' in '**p**ot' and 'h' in '**h**ot') on another day, pick out rhyming words, such as 'hot' and 'pot' in the rhyme 'Pease porridge hot'. 'Pot' and 'hot' are cvc words (consonant, vowel, consonant). Children are not naturally drawn to doing this and will usually be attracted, instead, by the initial sound and the rhyming chunk. Poetry cards give an embedded context that makes 'human sense' to them. But they also keep pressure from children if they are not ready for this. They can enjoy the rhyme story and characters, which will engage them with literature (hopefully for life).

Poetry cards give children anchor points

Children begin to pick out letters/graphemes they know

By the time the children are introduced to the second poetry card, they may well be beginning to pick out the letters they know, such as 'p' and 'h'.

Children begin to pick out the rhyming chunks they find

They will begin to see what the 'p' says, and what the 'j' says in 'pig' and 'jig'. As Karmiloff-Smith (1992) notes, children are both problem-solvers and problem-generators. They revel in being both, and are definitely not just passive receivers of what we wish to teach them. Instead they are active learners, using us as anchors, guides and resources.

They like the idea that you can break up words and then make them again

Some children will be able to segment the words 'pot' and 'hot' into their sounds, and blend the sounds 'p', 'h', 'o' and 't' into the words 'pot' and 'hot'. They can see that they can be reversed too. However, in order to do this children must understand the relationship between parts and whole. This is usually established by the age of six or seven years.

They begin to see that words stand for things

The picture of the pig, on the poetry card, will help them to remember that pig begins with a 'p'. Having picture cards, word cards and letter cards to go with a poetry card is very helpful too. Captions can also be helpful with having one line of the poetry card on a strip of card helping children to pick out the words. They will often seek out different aspects to focus on as they engage spontaneously with these play props.

They begin to realize that they need connecting words

As they play with the words from the poetry card, they will have some left over which do not go with pictures in the way 'pot' goes with the picture of the pot. These words are 'and', 'to', and so on. They are what Ragnarsdottir calls 'connecting words'.

Children will begin spontaneously to choose to play with the words and props around the poetry cards

In this book, many examples have been given of ways to enhance the processes of literacy. The mark-making area is invaluable. So, too, are the many games that children enjoy that use written words in ways which connect with the poetry cards. Sets of alphabets give other children great satisfaction, and also give them opportunities to blend and segment words. Sharing books and picking out interesting things to say about the text fascinates others. It is very important that the indoor and outdoor learning environments open up different aspects of the world of communication, language and literacy in a huge variety of ways.

Given that each child is unique, it goes without saying that children will respond and engage with these in their own way (Ellis, in Goouch and Lambirth,

2007). What is important is that they can find ways that are right for them, and get the help they need when they need it.

Encourage spontaneous opportunities for children to follow through on the essentials of literacy through poetry cards

- Leave props around for children to use with the rhyme.
- Make full use of everyday experiences to raise children's awareness, and to help them make links. They will soon begin to pick out letters in their name, or letters at the beginning of words on the poetry card, and to say the sounds. Opportunities arise in the garden, throughout the day, at toilet and snack times, at the computer, during group times, and when looking at environmental print and sharing stories.
- Make a rhyme box with the children. In an earlier chapter, we looked at the importance of pattern and how it helps the brain to make sense of many aspects of life, including reading and writing. Children love to see the patterns in rhyme, and will appreciate adults who help them to do this.

There is a wealth of research (including classic studies by Clay, 1998; Goddard-Blythe, 2004; Blakemore and Frith, 2005; Goswami, 2007; Snowling and Hulme, 2007) which points to reading and writing being complex processes in development and learning, involving use by the brain of integrating strategies. Don Holdaway (1979: 97), a pioneer in the teaching of reading and writing, suggests that 'Separate skills taught separately tend to be used separately by children'. Using the approach of this book builds the essentials of communication, language and literacy and avoids this problem. It is crucial that this continues until seven years of age. Poetry cards bridge the shift from phonemic awareness towards the alphabetic principle of mapping sounds onto letters and clusters of letters. They are therefore very useful in Reception classes, and also in the first years of statutory schooling.

A Reception class teacher from Abbotsmede Community Primary School who attended the training outlined in the 'Introduction' to this book reflected on the way she worked as a result:

> I have included nursery rhymes, finger plays and action songs as part of circle times. I understood the importance of rhyme, rhythm, a steady beat and having fun with silly words as a social, vocal and interactive adult-led activity. I feel I have greater understanding, and I have seen how my implementation of this knowledge has empowered the young children in my group to be emergent readers for their Reception year.
>
> It began with careful planning of small groups and an enabling environment where children can *listen* and not just hear. I found it essential to have as many props on board to help the children with English as an Additional Language access the circle times for maximum uptake. Once the children's focus was attained, it became a shared time, and the planning was no longer needed in such detail, because I [had] set a path, and the children [had] directed the route.

Once the basic words and actions were established for each rhyme in the programme and the children were familiar with them, I was able to add in new games to enhance the activities. For example, I had a square shoe box that Mr Fox lived in. I would start by saying, 'Here is a box all square, not round! I wonder what Mr Fox has found?' The children would then chant, 'Mr Fox, please tell us do! Mr Fox, please tell us do!' Then I would give clues as to the nursery rhyme prop or character that was inside. This then progressed to the children asking me questions about the characteristics of the prop in the box.

Applying rhymes at many times through the nursery session, with names, snacks, etc. ensured that the children's confidence progressed and rhyming became a natural part of their conversation and play.

Just as it was important for the children and staff to be aware of the programme, so it was for the parents to feel included. With busy parents (mainly mothers) coming and going, it was hard to hold a conversation and not feel I was rushing or preaching. An opportunity arose when parents were invited in for celebrations at different points in the calendar, such as Mother's Day. The children quite naturally resumed their circle time positions and we began our repertoire. For those parents who could not attend the circle time was videoed and displayed using a laptop at the beginning and end of each session. The feedback from parents convinced me that the programme was being effective. I provided handouts of words and actions alongside for children and parents to use at home.

By continuously dripping in key words, role modelling, being ever creative, ensuring children's interests and schemas were used productively, inviting parents in to join the group, involving other members of staff and making sure the circle times were upbeat, enjoyable and at all times silly, I feel that this year the children are better able to absorb letters and sounds in their Reception year.

This September some of the children that I worked with in the nursery will be part of my Reception class. Having participated in the CLLD programme [*outlined in this book*], I have planned and set up the area in the classroom for the poetry cards, related props, books, games and a collection of child friendly nursery rhyme books. I intend to revisit the nursery rhymes they are familiar with and introduce them to new members of the class. Having discussed the programme with the other Reception class teachers, we have agreed that the children will have a superb stepping stone [by] which to move into Phase 2 of letters and sounds.

The carefully thought-out programme, introducing children to the essentials of communication, language and literacy through a rich environment, packed with what Clay calls 'literacy events', offered in an unpressured way the help children required in their learning journey across the first five or more years. There was a continuity of approach, and parents were included throughout.

Why use poetry cards? Syllables, rhyming chunks, phonemic awareness

Having introduced the practicalities of how to make and introduce poetry cards in the first part of the chapter, it is now important to explore what exactly these contribute to helping a child to continue their journey deeper and deeper into literacy.

In any language there are three phonological grain sizes (syllables, rhyming chunks and phonemes). The phonology of a language is about the sounds of that language. In different ways each of these helps children to hear and identify the sounds making up words in English. We are concentrating on English in this chapter because children living in the four countries of the UK will be taught to read and write in English. Many children living in the UK will also be taught to read and write in other languages in addition to English, and this is to be encouraged. In many countries of the world it is normal to speak, read and write in three or more languages.

Developmentally across the world all children establish an awareness of syllables (the word 'di-no-saur' has three syllables, for example), then rhyming chunks (sing, spring), and last – and usually only with direct teaching – phonemic awareness (the smallest sounds in the word, 's-ee'). Research suggests that all three are important and develop in that order (English – Bradley and Bryant, 1983; Danish – Lundberg et al., 1988; German – Schneider et al., 1997).

Throughout the world children develop a sense of the syllable and rhyming chunks if they engage and participate in experiences that encourage this. But research has shown (see Goswami, in Goouch and Lambirth, 2007) they do not usually become aware of phonemes unless taught to do so. This is typically at the age of six or seven years. Phonemic awareness (the third grain size) is where the differences in our diverse languages can be seen most clearly. It seems likely that the same methods for teaching children to read and write will not be appropriate for all countries.

In languages where children develop phonemic awareness most easily there is great consistency and similarity between the way that syllables are segmented, rhyming chunks, and the way that phonemes are segmented. In many languages there are also many words of the cv type ('go', 'see'), but this is not the case in English, where only 5% of words are cv (De Cara and Goswami, 2002). Instead, English has many ccvc, cvc and cvcc words.

English is one of the most irregular and inconsistent languages in the world

In languages other than English (Goswami, 2005), it often makes sense to teach children to read and write with an emphasis on synthetic phonics. Some languages are phonologically consistent, with a consonant-vowel (cv) syllable structure (for example, Italian, Spanish and Chinese), while in some others a letter or letter cluster will always be pronounced in the same way (Italian, Spanish and Greek). Some languages have consistency in the spelling of the written language (Italian). Italian is consistent in all these respects.

In light of this it seems understandable and natural that the pioneer educator Maria Montessori (as an Italian) argued for synthetic phonics as the prime approach to teaching children to read and write. In languages with an almost 1:1 correspondence when mapping sounds onto letters, it makes sense to teach mainly through the synthetic phonics strategy.

However, children learning to read and write in English will face two hurdles:

- English is very inconsistent in its orthography (how it is written down)
- English is very complex phonologically (how it sounds).

'English is an exceptionally inconsistent alphabetic language because it suffers from a large amount of inconsistency in both reading and writing' (Goswami, 2005: 274). But it is interesting to see that even in those countries where phonemic awareness is straightforward because it corresponds with the orthography (how it is written down) and maps the sounds onto the letters (Turkish, Greek, German, Spanish and Italian), children are not usually taught to read and write until they are six or seven years old. At this age they can learn quickly and easily, typically in about three months. The brain is ready and they will have built up those language experiences which will aid the brain, and indeed sculpt the established language processes into a further symbolic wave and function, adding the layer of reading and writing.

Mapping sounds onto letters

English, as we have seen throughout the book, is a very inconsistent language. It is not consistent in its phonology (the sounds of the language) and neither is it so in the way it is written down (the orthography). The words 'though', 'through', 'cough' and 'bough' look similar, but sound quite different when they are spoken. The words 'cape', 'chalk' and 'tar' all have an 'a' in the middle, but it sounds quite different in each word when spoken. Children learning to read and write in English need to use a whole range of strategies in parallel if they are going to manage to decode what is written and to read it, or if they are going to compose a piece of writing and encode the sounds into written words. They need to be able to recognize words like 'yacht' by developing some sight vocabulary. They need to tackle irregular words with rhyming chunks, through recognizing the bits which rhyme as a pattern but can't be worked out by using other strategies, such as 'sight', 'light' and 'night'. Last, and most difficult, they need to map sounds onto letters to read regular words such as 'dog' and 'cat'.

Children learning to read and write in languages like Spanish, Finnish, Italian and German don't have to do this. They simply have to learn to map phonemes (the smallest sounds in the words) and graphemes (the clusters of letters making the sound) and see the phoneme/grapheme correspondence in order to be effective readers. The synthetic phonics method works for almost every word in these languages. But children will not be expected to do this until they are about six or seven.

Research shows that children learning to read and write in English will typically problem-solve in reading by using their knowledge of rhyming chunks. Children learning to read and write in English find it harder to read longer words and non-words using synthetic phonics as a strategy. Research by others (Schneider et al. 1997; Snow, 2006; Frith, et al. 1998; Goswami, in Goouch and Lambirth; 2007) shows that they typically tackle this by reading a non-word using the seeming chunk phonics strategy. If they know the word 'pot' they will work out how to read 'dot'. If it is a nonsense word they will use their knowledge of the word 'six' to work out and read 'tix'. They will often experiment and giggle (particularly six- and seven-year-olds) as they spontaneously make up nonsense words that rhyme. This is a natural way in which children practise the rhyming chunk strategy and get to grips with this grain of phonological awareness.

What does research evidence as well as the experience of teachers tell us?

Different methods of teaching children to read come into and go out of fashion, but the best teaching is done when teachers know their children, informed by their observations of them, and really tune into what each child needs in terms of active adult help and support. In order to do this, practitioners need to know about how children develop and learn, and they also need to be aware of the essentials of learning to read and write.

Remarkable claims have been made recently for the synthetic phonics method (Johnston and Watson, 2004; Rose Review, 2006; Centre for Policy Studies, Gross, 2010). Here Wyse and Goswami (2008) have found the evidence does not stand up to scrutiny, as most of the studies have not used robust research methods. They found that the following used robust research methods.

Landerl (2000) has suggested that children taught using mixed methods performed almost as well as children taught through phonics only. In a controlled study Walton et al. (2001) compared synthetic and analytic phonic methods, and found the only difference was that children taught through analytic phonics did better in word reading. Spencer and Hanley (in Goouch and Lambirth, 2003) studied bilingual six-year-old Welsh children, who were either taught to read in English or in Welsh using a synthetic phonics programme. They found that children who were learning to read and write in English made many more errors in both word and no-word reading than the children who were learning to read and write in Welsh. This means that the difficulties children face (in learning to read and write in English with orthography and phonology) make it more difficult to learn using synthetic phonics only than in Welsh which is more regular in both.

The US National Reading Panel (2000) study indicates that phonics teaching contributes to children learning to read in important ways. This has not been doubted by effective teachers, who instinctively tailor their teaching to the individual needs of children. Some children respond better to phonics teaching and others to analytic methods. An important observational study by Chittenden, Salinger and Bussis (2001) showed that some children are anxious to keep hold of the meaning of what they read, and will therefore guess words from contexts and make errors which are then self corrected as part of that process. Other children drilled down to get the word right, and were in danger of losing the flow. Different children need a different emphasis in the help they are given, and good teachers will draw on a range of strategies and use their experience as they teach.

Most children, at the age of six or seven years, in most countries of the world, will begin to read and write without difficulty. History has shown it seems that from the 1870s when mass education developed in the UK that between 15 and 20% of children have had difficulty in learning to read and write. Of these, some will never do so (for example, children with disabilities may not). With careful and appropriate skilled and trained teaching some children with learning difficulties will learn to read later, perhaps even in adolescence. Children with visual impairments, especially progressive conditions, will learn to read and write in Braille, a skill usually best developed at about seven years of age. Children with a language delay and hearing loss will usually read later than this. But the narrowness of vocabulary can make this a difficult task until the middle years of childhood (8–12 years). Children learning to read and write in a second language will be in a very strong position as they go through their education and life only if they are encouraged to learn, and in an unpressured way, as they distinguish between the two languages.

The development of the human brain is such that during the first five years there is major development in non-verbal communication (which remains 85% of our communication throughout life), language and other kinds of symbol systems (music, dance), made possible by the development of memory, imagination (remembering images and reassembling them in new and fascinating ways), pretending, and creating by making new connections. The best time to teach children to read comes once these processes have been well established, serving as a rich foundation. This is typically at about age six to seven. It is interesting to note that in most countries this is indeed the age at which reading and writing are taught.

Research by Snow (2006) is in line with this. It shows that while phonological skills in children at the age of five years do act as better predictors of reading at that age, having a good vocabulary at age five is a better predictor of how children will achieve more complex reading tasks, including comprehension (understanding what they read), by the time they leave primary school. This resonates closely with the findings of Ragnarsdottir (2006), who also found that children who had made stories in their spontaneous play, and who had acted out stories that were read to them, could better achieve in reading and writing tasks, including comprehension and word recognition, by eleven years of age.

Similarly, the Scale Point Study (based on Local Authority results across England of the *Early Years Foundation Stage Profile*, 2008), showed that the high level of competence in children's use of phonics in spelling and their ability to write sentences with punctuation at five years of age was not vital for attaining a Level 3 at the end of Key Stage 1 in the English system. Just over half of the children who attained a Level 3 in writing had gained these points.

Recognizing words and understanding what they mean

Gough and Tunmer (1986), who influenced the 'Simple approach to reading' in the Rose Review (Rose, 2006), believe that word recognition means the ability to recognize words presented singly out of context. They argue that the only way children can do this in a context-free situation is to use phonic rules. But they also argue that word recognition supports meaning-making, understanding and comprehension.

Jeni Riley (2007: 82) emphasizes the need to bring these together, showing that both speedy and automatic decoding and understanding of what the word means are important in learning to read and write: 'Practitioners who are aware of the multifacetness of the literacy process are more able to provide a variety of appropriate teaching approaches for their pupils' (Riley, 2007: 83).

Showing very young children words and letters in isolation isolates them from context. Poetry cards allow children to bring linguistic meaning to a text through alliteration, rhyme and rhythm, which is a natural process for them. These open the way for them to engage with the 'givens' (phonic work), which are less natural for the human brain (Carter, 1999: 153). Marian Whitehead (2007: 53) warns against concentrating on the 'surface bits', such as correct letter formation or reciting letter sounds, which neglect, she argues, the real literacy basics. It is important not to undermine what she calls 'home literacies and meaningful engagements with books and literature'.

Sue Palmer and Ros Bayley emphasize this in their seven strands that make up the *Foundations of Literacy*: 'The importance of language in education cannot be exaggerated. It is the bedrock on which all formal learning is based, not least the learning of literacy skills' (2004: 7).

The strands they identify as appropriate for 3–6-year-olds, which fit comfortably with this book, are:

- learning to listen
- time to talk
- music, movement and memory
- storytime
- learning about print
- tuning into sound
- moving into writing.

'Pushing a child toward a new skill too soon can cut short the preceding period of organisation and preparation, which provides the basis for later automatisation of functioning' (Goddard-Blythe, 2004: 48).

Understanding comes before competence

Children know more than they can tell us, and we must not underestimate them. Children should not be put under inappropriate pressure to learn to read and write, but at the same time it is important that we actively help children to become aware of what Dame Marie Clay calls 'literacy situations' before they are able to be explicit about them: 'Literacy enthusiasts are in danger of narrowing the interpretation of what contributes to school progress, while early childhood educators are in danger of setting literacy aside until children get to school' (Clay, 1998: 12–20).

She suggests that opening up the world of literacy to children is developed by:

- actively providing opportunities for children to notice literacy events
- observing how children show us their literacy awareness
- seizing opportunities to interact with children as they show us their literacy awareness
- opening up further opportunities for literacy learning (communication, language developments, spontaneous free-flow play [see Bruce, 1991; 2004b; Bruce et al., 2010] developments, reading developments, and writing developments).

Making human sense of reading and writing

Margaret Donaldson points out that when learning makes 'human sense' to children, they can tackle more difficult ideas. When children are in content-free situations, they cannot bring meaning to what they have been asked to do.

Content-free situations mean that children cannot naturally connect with what Margaret Donaldson calls the 'givens' of a task. In this case the task is a literacy one, of making grapheme/phoneme correspondences, segmenting and the blending, and then reversing these: 'it is of the essence of these kind of problems that you are required to stick to the given. The problem is to be taken as encapsulated, isolated from the rest of a existence' (Donaldson, 1978: 200).

Two things need to be in place if children are going to connect with the 'givens' of a move from phonemic awareness to reading texts and writing:

- Children need rich learning environments which are content-full and not content-free. Poetry cards supply this.
- Children need to spend time with adults who know about development and learning as well as the structures and systems that are central to developing literacy. They can then offer the right help at the right time in the right way.

Word comprehension depends on good language development, discourse proficiency and vocabulary. Linguistic processes contribute to our comprehension of talking, listening, reading and writing

Using everyday situations to bridge the gap into less natural learning – environmental print

At first, children will be encouraged to 'have a go' at begining to problem-solve their way into texts (Chittenden et al., 2007). They use the signs and clues they find in the context, such as the rhymes in familiar and regularly used poetry cards. This gives them confidence and shows them strategies that can be useful in the early stages of engaging with text. Poetry cards help adults to help children learn the strategies that will help them towards later phonic work, so that they can have a go at words whether or not these are in a context.

In everyday life there is not often a need to read a single word out of context. 'EXIT', 'TOILET', or 'SALE' signs are examples of this, but often environmental print will carry captions – 'THIS WAY TO THE MUSEUM', 'NO PARKING'. The context prevents a meaningless isolation of the words and helps the emergent and beginner reader to recognize and understand particular words.

Environmental print is important as it gives children small chunks of print, and sometimes words in isolation, but within a meaningful context. They can then use these as a way to build a sight vocabulary with confidence and pleasure

The child's name

The letters that children learn most readily are those imbued with meaning.

A form of print likely to elicit letter processing is that of personal names. Bloodgood (1999) studied 3–5 year olds. Although the youngest children knew only a few letters and could read few if any preprimer words, they could recognize their own names in isolation and sometimes names of their classmates. Children's comments suggested that initial letters were the salient cues remembered. Also, knowledge of the letters in their own names accounted for most of the letters they could identify. (Ehri, in Snowling and Hulme, 2007: 141)

Much-loved poetry cards also help children to engage with texts in meaningful ways.

Print should be placed in a meaningful context – 'Hang up your coat'. This notice has a function. It is not just there as as decoration, with little purpose or meaning

We have looked at the importance of the child's name, and other special words throughout the book

In what order should children be introduced to the linking of sounds with letters?

The alphabetic principle, all experts agree, is important in the learning of reading and writing. It involves the linking of sounds and letters so that children can learn about the way that the smallest units of sound (phonemes) map onto letters in words. The letters might be single ones (pot, p-o-t; hot, h-o-t), or clusters (bell, b-e-ll; shell, sh-e-ll). These are called graphemes.

Once phonemic awareness has been established, children will, with help, begin to enjoy blending and segmenting words. This means that when they pick out a word like 'hot' on a poetry card, they can blend the sounds h-o-t in order to say 'hot'. They can say a word like 'pot' and write down or find the letters for each sound to make the word. On the whole this phase is best matched with children aged six and seven. However, there will be a significant minority of children who will not yet be able to use these strategies. They may:

- have a learning difficulty
- have a disability
- be a new arrival in England and new to the sounds of the English language
- learn English as an additional language
- have experienced physical and emotional abuse, and so need experiences that open up communication, language and play, with pleasure in being read to by a summer-born child
- simply need more time (which in most parts of the world is the norm).

Initial sounds

Children naturally look at initial and end sounds before paying attention to the middle of words. We taught the children the initial sounds so that they would learn the strategies needed to do this.

Because we used only two carefully chosen rhymes, we regularly repeated the rhyming chunks with the children. We displayed the rhyme so that children's attention was drawn to the look of the patterns which occur in the look of the words that rhymed. We used this as background support to the teaching of the initial grapheme/phoneme correspondences, but only if appropriate for individual children.

This process is appropriate for children who are mainly in statutory schooling. For a few younger children we could show how to segment and blend and reverse these in relation to 'p' and 'h' with 'hot' and 'pot'. In the second poetry card we introduced 'pig' and 'jig'. We found the children used the rhyme to help them.

The importance of a rich learning environment

The emphasis on a rich, multi-sensory language environment means that children are encouraged in a variety of ways to tune into the sounds of English. The poetry cards provide a supportive backcloth, which helps children to map the sounds (phonemes) onto the graphemes, supported by the alliteration of initial sounds, syllabification and rhyming chunks. Using poetry cards avoids drilling children, and makes this an enjoyable, comfortable experience with literacy. These enrich a child's understanding and engagement with literature. This encourages the systematic teaching of GPC (Grapheme/Phoneme Correspondence) rules and phoneme segmentation and blending against a backcloth of rich language and the supportive sound patterns of rhyme. However doing this does not neglect the uniqueness of each child.

The canon of traditional nursery rhymes and stories, as well as modern songs, poems and stories with rhyming phrases and refrains, helps this aspect (Barrs and Meek, 2007). Many children will not have had the kinds of experiences that develop these skills. Yet this is a crucial part of phonics training in a child's education. It will bring together many aspects of learning as well as contributing to a lifelong need and joy in reading and writing.

These three approaches (syllabification, rhyming chunks and phonemic awareness) are important when using the poetry cards and mapping the sounds onto the written print. It is important that adults:

'Run, run as fast as you can, You can't catch me, I'm the gingerbread man'

- alongside this use alliteration and rhyming chunks so that children can actively seek out the patterns in letters and sounds of words, a process which comes naturally to them. Alliteration encourages children to work through the word from left to right
- encourage children in what they naturally do, in looking at initial sounds and rhyming chunks, but show them how to blend and segment regular cvc words
- help children with the 'tricky' words which must be learnt as a whole as sight vocabulary (for example, 'choir', 'yacht').

Children who have learned to listen to the sounds in words will get more out of rhymes. This in turn feeds into their possibility to enjoy rhyming strings, and to segment and blend. It is a virtuous circle. But rushing children is a mistake.

Make sure you know the technical literacy jargon, but take care not to exclude parents

Jargon often excludes people, so it is important that as practitioners we should try to feel comfortable with recently introduced literacy jargon and find ways to share it with parents in an accessible way. It is very unfortunate that in the past decade the language has become so technical. It is sad to think that the development of communication, language and literacy could be hampered because practitioners, parents and grandparents are required to develop an unfamiliar vocabulary around such an important aspect of children's development and learning. In a group interview with professional working parents, Kathy Goouch in Goouch and Lambirth, (2007) found that they did not know what the technical terms meant. What mattered to them was that their children enjoyed books, and had a love of stories and finding things out. They delighted in observing the imaginative and problem-solving strategies their children employed in tackling print, and in their attempts to make sense of reading and writing. Above all they did not want to see all of that destroyed through dreary, pedestrian formal lessons or drill teaching. They were anxious that the good start their children had made would continue, and feared that children who had not learned to enjoy books would be at a disadvantage, and would not find formal teaching easy or enjoyable.

Explaining something in simple words is a very good way of making sure you really understand it. If you cannot explain to a colleague, parent or carer the meanings of 'phoneme', 'grapheme', 'blending' and 'segmenting', then you do not understand the subject matter. If you do not understand, you should not introduce poetry cards.

IN SUMMARY

Poetry cards depend on communication, language and experience in the early years of life. They need careful introduction if they are to engage a diverse range of children, but the effort of introducing them in ways right for each unique child brings rewards.

- Seeing the poetry cards that adults have made encourages children to make their own cards, and to have a go at writing.
- They give children an important part of the time-honoured canon of literature in English culture, helping them to tune into those sounds, rhythms and cadences of the English language that are essential to fluent reading and writing.
- The literary themes of the poems chosen are cross-cultural (eating, falling down, tending growing plants, and so on).

- Poetry cards, in important ways, offer children the technical help they need in order to read and write in English.
- They help children to link with other areas of development and learning.

There is a growing tendency in England to focus, not on the 80% of children who learn to read without difficulty by the age of six or seven, or on the 5% of children who for good reasons will never learn to read because of disabilities of complex kinds, but instead to headline the 15%–20% or so of children who find it difficult to learn to read. The main reason for such difficulties is that they have a lack of experiences of the important kind (Snow, 2006) compared with the 80% who learn to read easily. Instead of beginning with the deficiencies in the system, it is better to start with the strengths, and to see what makes children find learning to read and write an exciting adventure that will remain with them throughout their lives. Establishing good communication and language development, and having interesting and enriching experiences which are brought to bear on texts, and are a resource to write about, are the essential foundations for learning to read and write.

Reading and writing help children to participate fully in their family life (writing to grandma, thanking people, etc.), their community (writing a letter to campaign against a tree in the street being cut down), and gradually the wider cultural, economic and political life of the nation. The process of writing helps with the formation of arguments, and reading informs and takes the imagination forward, leading to creativity. Reading and writing give a sense of personal fulfilment, and as thoughts and feelings, ideas and relationships are put onto paper they are clarified and become more articulate and better argued than when left in the mind. From birth children are part of their culture and community, and will actively participate in literary events if given the opportunities to do so.

KEY TERMS

Alphabetic principle – this is about the way sounds and letters link. Sounds can be represented by writing one of the 26 letters of the alphabet, or by a cluster of letters. Because there are 44 sounds in the English language, there are not enough letters to represent each sound. All experts agree that it is important for children to understand the links between letters and sounds

Analytic phonics – this approach to phonics helps children to look for patterns in words which have larger chunks than phonemes

Blending – this involves building the separate sounds up into a word in order, all through the word. It is useful for regular words

cvc words – consonant, vowel, consonant

(Continued)

(Continued)

GPC – grapheme/phoneme correspondence

Grapheme – the letter or cluster of letters representing a sound

Phoneme – the smallest unit of sound in a word

Rhyming chunks – pig, jig, in 'To Market, to Market, to Buy a Fat Pig'

Segmenting – this involves separating out the sounds in a word that is regular

Syllable – this is part of a word which is pronounced as one beat. For example, 'porridge' is two syllables (two beats) in the rhyme 'Pease Porridge Hot'. Clapping the beat of children's names is a popular way for them to enjoy working out the number of syllables in a word

Synthetic phonics – this is one kind of phonics. It is based on the belief that reading is a simple matter of decoding and encoding. It emphasizes the regular words, describing those that do not follow the rules as 'tricky' words. These have to be learnt as 'sight vocabulary'

Reading

Bruce, T., Meggitt, C. and Grenier, J. (2010) *Childcare and Education* (5th edn). London: Hodder Arnold.

Further Reading

Chittenden, E. and Salinger, T. with Bussis, A. (2001) *Inquiry into Meaning: An Investigation of Learning to Read,* (revised edn, with an introduction by D. Meier). New York and London: Teachers College Press.
Clay, M. (1998) 'From acts to awareness in early literacy', *Children's Issues,* 2 (1): 12–20.
Wyse, D. and Goswami, U. (2008) 'Synthetic phonics and the teaching of reading', *British Educational Research Journal,* 34, (6) December: 691–710.

Bibliography

Abbott, L. and Langston, A. (eds) (2006) *Parents Matter*. Maidenhead: Open University Press/McGraw-Hill.

Adams, M. (1990) *Beginning to Read: Thinking and Learning about Print*. Cambridge, MA: MIT Press.

Ashton-Warner, S. (1965) *Teacher*. New York: Simon & Schuster.

Baddeley, P. and Eddershaw, C. (1994) *Not So Simple Picture Books: Developing Responses to Literature with 4–12 Year Olds*. Stoke-on-Trent: Trentham Books.

Barrs, M. and Meek, M. (2007) 'Inquiry into meaning: a conversation' in K. Goouch and A. Lambirth (eds), *Understanding Phonics and the Teaching of Reading: Critical Perspectives*. Maidenhead: Open University Press/McGraw-Hill Education.

Bartholomew, L. and Bruce, T. (1993) *Getting to Know You: A Guide to Record-Keeping in Early Childhood Education*. London: Hodder & Stoughton.

Basic Skills Agency (BSA) (2005) *Language and Play*. London: BSA.

Bateson, G. (1995, 1976) 'A theory of play and fantasy', in J. Bruner, A. Jolly and K. Sylva (eds) *Play: Its Role in Development and Evolution*. New York: Basic Books.

Bayley, R. and Broadbent, L. (2004) *Helping Children with Special Beat*. Birmingham: Lawrence Educational Publications.

Bialystok, E. (1991) 'Letters, sounds and symbols: changes in children's understanding of written language', *Applied Psycholinguistics*, 12: 75–89.

Bissex, G. (1980) *GYNS AT WRK (GENIUS AT WORK: A Child Learns to Write and Read)*. Cambridge, MA: MIT Press.

Blakemore, C. (2001) 'What makes a developmentally appropriate early childhood curriculum?', lecture given at the Royal Society of Arts, 14 February.

Blakemore, S.J. and Frith, U. (2005) *The Learning Brain: Lessons for Education*. Oxford: Blackwell.

Bloodgood, J. (1999) 'What's in a name? Children's name writing and name acquisition', *Reading Research Quarterly*, 34: 342–67.

Bradley, L. and Bryant, P. (1983) 'Categorising sounds and learning to read: a causal connection', *Nature*, 10: 419–21.

Bradley, L. and Bryant, P. (1988) 'Rhyme and reason in reading and spelling', International Academy for Research in Learning Difficulties, monograph series, no. 1. Ann Arbor, MI: University of Michigan Press.

Brice-Heath, S. (1983) *Ways with Words: Life, Language and Work in Communities and Classrooms.* Cambridge: Cambridge University Press.

Britton, J. (1970) *Language and Learning.* London: Allen Lane.

Brooke, L. (2002) *Starting School: Young Children Learning Cultures.* Maidenhead: Open University Press/McGraw-Hill.

Brown, G. (2007) The Mansion House Speech, City Hall, London, 20 June.

Browne, A. (2001) *Developing Language and Literacy 3–8* (2nd edn). London: Paul Chapman Publishing.

Bruce, T. (1991) *Time to Play in Early Childhood Education and Care.* London: Hodder & Stoughton.

Bruce, T. (2001) *Learning Through Play: Babies, Toddlers and the Foundation Years.* London: Hodder/Arnold.

Bruce, T. (2004a) *Cultivating Creativity: Babies, Toddlers and the Early Years.* London: Hodder/Arnold.

Bruce, T. (2004b) *Developing Learning in Early Childhood.* London: Paul Chapman Publishing.

Bruce, T. (2005a) 'Editor's notes', *Early Childhood Practice: The Journal for Multi-Professional Partnerships,* 7: 17–20.

Bruce, T. (2005b) *Early Childhood Education* (3rd edn). London: Hodder/Arnold.

Bruce, T. (2010) *Early Childhood: A Guide for Students* (2nd edn). London: SAGE.

Bruce, T., Grenier, J. and Meggitt, C. (2010) *Childcare and Education* (5th edn). London: Hodder/Arnold.

Bruner, J. (1977) *The Process of Education* (2nd edn). Cambridge, MA, and London: Harvard University Press.

Bryant, P. and Bradley, L. (1985) *Children's Reading Problems.* Oxford: Blackwell.

Buckley, B. (2003) *Children's Communication Skills from Birth to Five Years.* Abingdon: Routledge.

Bullock, A. (1975) *A Language for Life: The Bullock Report.* London: HMSO.

Carter, R. (1999) *Mapping the Mind.* London: Seven Dials, Orion.

Chittenden, E. and Salinger, T. with Bussis, A. (2001) *Inquiry into Meaning: An Investigation of Learning to Read,* revised edn, with an introduction by D.Meier, New York and London: Teachers College Press.

Christie, J. (ed.) (1991) *Play and Early Literacy Development.* Albany, NY: State University of New York Press.

Chukovsky, K. (1963) *From Two to Five.* Berkeley, CA: University of California Press.

Clarke, M. (1976) *Young Fluent Readers: What Can They Teach Us?* London: Heinemann.

Clay, M. (1975) *What Did I Write?* London: Heinemann.

Clay, M. (1982) *Observing Young Readers – Selected Readings.* Portsmouth, NH: Heinemann.

Clay, M. (1986) *Reading: The Patterning of Complex Behaviour* (3rd edn). Auckland: Heinemann.

Clay, M. (1993) *An Observational Survey of Early Literacy Development.* Portsmouth, NH: Heinemann.

Clay, M. (1998) 'From acts to awareness in early literacy', *Children's Issues,* 2 (1): 12–20.

Coltheart, M. (2007) 'Modeling reading: the dual-route approach', in M. Snowling and C. Hulme (eds), *The Science of Reading.* Oxford; Malden, MA and Carlton, Victoria: Blackwell.

Creating the Picture (2009) (only available on the web. This can be downloaded from www.standards.dcsf.gov.uk/primary.publications/foundation_stage/creating-picture and the reference is: 00283-2007DWO-EN-01.)

Crystal, D. (2006) *Words, Words, Words*. Oxford: Oxford University Press.

Damasio, A. (2004) *Looking for Spinoza*. London: Random House.

De Cara, B. and Goswami, U. (2002) Statistical analysis of similarity relations among spoken words: evidence for the special status of rimes, *English Behavioural Research Methods and Instrumentation*, 34 (3): 416–23.

Department for Education and Employment (DfEE) (1997) *The Implementation of the National Literacy Strategy: Final Report*. London: Department for Education and Employment.

Department for Education and Employment (DfEE) (1998) *The National Literacy Strategy: Framework for Teaching*. London: DfEE.

Department for Education and Skills (DfES) (2005a) *Communicating Matters: The Strands of Communication and Language*. London: DfES.

Department for Education and Skills (DfES) (2005b) *Early Reading Development Pilot – Consultant File*. London: DfES.

Department for Education and Skills (DfES) (2006a) *Independent Review of the Teaching of Reading: Final Report*. Nottingham: DfES. Crown Copyright.

Department for Education and Skills (DfES) (2006b) *Seamless Transitions – Supporting Continuity in Young Children's Learning*. London: DfES.

Department for Education and Skills (DfES) (Togerson, C.J., Brooks, G. and Hall, J.) (2006c) *A Systematic Review of the Research Literature on the Use of Phonics in the Teaching of Reading and Spelling*. London: DfES.

Department for Education and Skills (DfES) (2007a) *Early Years Foundation Stage*. London: DfES.

Department for Education and Skills (DfES) (2007b) *Letters and Sounds: Principles and Practice of High Quality Phonics*. London: DfES.

Department for Education and Skills (DfES) (2007c) 'Creating the Picture' (available on the web only: www.standards.dcsf.gov.uk/primary/publications/foundation_stage/creating_picture/. Reference: 00283-2007DWO-EN-01).

Department for Education and Skills/Qualifications and Curriculum Authority (DfES/QCA) (2000) *Curriculum Guidance for the Foundation Stage*. London: DfES.

Department for Education and Skills/Qualifications and Curriculum Authority (DfES/QCA) (2003) *Foundation Stage Profile Handbook*. London: DfES.

Dombey, H. (2006) 'How should we teach children to read?', *Books for Keeps*, 156: 6–7.

Donaldson, M. (1978) *Children's Minds*. London: Fontana/Collins.

Dowling, M. (2010) *Young Children's Personal, Social and Emotional Development* (3rd edn). London: SAGE.

Dunn, O. (2007) 'Books for birth to threes', *Nursery World*, June.

Dunne, J. (1988) *The Beginnings of Social Understanding*. Oxford: Blackwell.

Edgington, M. (2004) *The Foundation Teacher in Action: Teaching 3, 4 and 5 Year Olds* (3rd edn). London: Paul Chapman Publishing/SAGE.

Edwards, C., Gandini, L. and Forman, G. (1998) *The Hundred languages of Children*. Westport, CT and London: Ablex.

Ehri, L. (2007) 'Development of sight word reading: phases and findings', in M. Snowling and C. Hulme (eds), *The Science of Reading*. Oxford; Malden, MA and Carlton, Victoria: Blackwell.

Ellis, M. (1992) 'Tempo perception and performance of elementary students in grades 3–6', *Journal of Research in Music Education*, 40 (41): 329–41.

Ellis, S. (2006) 'A response to Stuart', *The Psychology of Education Review*, 30 (2): 21–2.

Featherstone, S. (ed.) (2006) *L is for Sheep: Getting Ready for Phonics*. Cambridge: Lutterworth Press.

Ferreiro, E. (1997) 'Writing and thinking about writing systems', *Conference Lectures on Literacy: From Research to Practice*. London: Institute of Education.

Feynman, R. (1990) *What Do You Care What Other People Think? Further Adventures of a Curious Character*. London: Unwin Hyman.

Frabetti, R. (2005) 'Eyes and silences', *Early Childhood Practice: The Journal for Multi-Professional Partnerships*, 7 (1): 63–72.

Frith, U., Wimmer, H. and Landerl, K. (1998) 'Differences in phonological recoding in German- and English–speaking children', *Scientific Studies of Reading*, 2: 31–99.

Froebel, F. (1887) *The Education of Man*. New York: Appleton.

Gamble, N. and Yates, S. (2008) *Exploring Children's Literature* (2nd edn). London: SAGE.

Gentry, J.R. (1982) 'An analysis of developmental spelling in GYNS AT WRK', *The Reading Teacher*, Nov: 192–200.

Goddard-Blythe, S. (2004) *The Well-Balanced Child – Movement and Early Learning*. Stroud: Hawthorn Press.

Goouch, K. (2007) 'Parents' voices: a conversation with parents of pre-school children', in K. Goouch and A. Lambirth (eds) *Understanding Phonics and the Teaching of Reading: Critical Perspectives*. Maidenhead: Open University Press/McGraw-Hill.

Goouch, K. and Lambirth, A. (eds) (2007) *Understanding Phonics and the Teaching of Reading: Critical Perspectives*. Maidenhead: Open University Press/McGraw-Hill.

Goswami, U. (1998) *Cognition in Children*. Hove: Psychology Press.

Goswami, U. (2005) 'Synthetic phonics and learning to read: a cross-cultural perspective', *Educational Psychology in Practice*, 21 (4): 273–82.

Goswami, U. (2006) 'Research evidence and teaching phonics: a response to Stuart', *The Psychology of Education Review*, 30 (2): 23–5.

Goswami, U. and Bryant, P. (1990) *Phonological Skills and Learning to Read*. Hove: Psychology Press.

Goswami, U. and Ziegler, J.C. (2006) 'A developmental perspective on the neural code for written words', *Trends in Cognitive Sciences*, 10 (4): 142–3.

Goswami, U. 'Learning to read across languages: the role of phonics and synthetic phonics', in K. Goouch and A. Lambirth (eds) (2007) *Understanding Phonics and the Teaching of Reading: Critical Perspectives*. Maidenhead: Open University Press/McGraw-Hill.

Gough, P. and Tunmer, W. (1986) 'Decoding, reading and reading disability', *Remedial and Special Education*, 7: 6–10.

Gove, M. (2010) *The Democratic Intellect – What do we Need to Succeed in the 21st Century?* Sir John Cass Foundation Lecture, December. London: Sir John Cass Foundation.

Greenland, P. (2006) 'Physical development', in T. Bruce (ed.), *Early Childhood: A Guide for Students*. London: SAGE.

Greenland, P. (2010) *Hopping Home Backwards: Body Intelligence and Movement Play* (2nd edn). Leeds: Jabadao/Reading.

Griffiths, N. (2001) *Storysacks*. Reading and Language Information Centre, University of Reading.

Gross, M. (2010) *So Why Can't They Read?* Surrey: Centre for Policy Studies.

Hall, K. (2007) 'Rose in context: the teaching of reading in initial teacher education', Keynote address at the Conference of the Universities Council for the Education of Teachers (UCET), London, 11 September.

Hall, K. 'To codify pedagogy or enrich learning? A Wengerian perspective on early literacy policy in England', in K. Goouch and A. Lambirth (eds) (2007) *Understanding Phonics and the Teaching of Reading: Critical Perspectives*. Maidenhead: Open University Press/ McGraw-Hill.

Hall, N. and Robinson, A. (1996) *Learning about Punctuation*. Clevedon, PA and Adelaide: Multilingual Matters.

Hall, N. and Robinson, A. (2003) *Exploring Writing and Play in the Early Years* (2nd edn). London: David Fulton.

Harrison, E. (1895) *A Study of Child Nature from the Kindergarten Standpoint*. New York and London: Garland. (Originally published by the Chicago Kindergarten College in 1895.)

Holdaway, D. (1979) *Foundations of Literacy*. London: Scholastic.

Hutchins, V. (2006) 'Meeting individual needs', in T. Bruce, *Early Childhood: A Guide for Students*. London: SAGE.

Johnson, R. and Watson, J. (2004) 'Accelerating the development of reading, spelling and phonemic awareness skills in initial readers', *Reading and Writing*, 17: 327–57.

Kalliala, M. (2005) *Play Culture in a Changing World*. Maidenhead: Open University Press/ McGraw-Hill.

Karmiloff-Smith, A. (1992) *Beyond Modularity: A Developmental Perspective on Cognitive Science*. Cambridge, MA: MIT Press/Bradford Books.

Kate Greenaway Nursery School and Children's Centre (2009) *Core Experiences for the Early Years Foundation Stage*.

Kuhlman, K. and Schweinhart, L. (1999) *Movement, Music and Timing*. Ypsilanti, MI: High Scope Educational Research Foundation.

Laevers, F. (1994) *The Innovative Project 'Experiential Education' and the Definition of Quality in Education*. Leuven: Katholieke Universiteit.

Landerl, K. (2000) 'Influences of orthographic consistency and reading instruction on the development of non-word reading skills', *European Journal of Psychology of Education*, 15: 239–57.

Langer, E. (1997) *The Power of Mindful Learning*. Harlow: Addison–Wesley.

Liebschner, J. (1992) *A Child's World: Freedom and Guidance in Froebel's Theory and Practice*. Oxford: Butterworth.

Lilley, J. (1967) *Friedrich Froebel: A Selection from his Writings*. Cambridge: Cambridge University Press.

Lundberg, I., Frost, J. and Petersen, O. (1988) 'Effects of an extensive programme for stimulating phonological awareness in pre-school children', *Reading Quarterly*, 23: 163–284.

MacIntyre, C. and McVitty, K. (2004) *Movement and Learning in the Early Years*. London: Paul Chapman Publishing.

Makin, L. and Whitehead, M. (2004) *How to Develop Children's Early Literacy: A Guide for Carers and Educators*. London: Paul Chapman Publishing.

Mallett, M. (2005) *The Primary English Encyclopaedia: The Heart of the Curriculum*. London: David Fulton.

Malloch, S. and Trevarthen, C. (2010) *Communicative Musicality: Exploring the Basis of Human Companionship*. Oxford: Oxford University Press.

Manguel, A. (1997) *A History of Reading*. London: Flamingo.

Marsh, J. and Hallett, E. (eds) (1999) *Desirable Literacies: Approaches to Language and Literacy in the Early Years*. London: Paul Chapman Publishing.

Matterson, E. (1991) *This Little Puffin: Finger Plays and Nursery Games*, London: Puffin.

Matthews, J. (2003) *Drawing and Painting: Children and Visual Representation* (2nd edn). London: Paul Chapman Publishing.

Meade, A. (2003) 'What are the implications of brain studies on early childhood education?', *Early Childhood Practice: The Journal for Multi-Professional Partnerships*, 5 (2): 4–18.

Meek, M. (1982) *Learning to Read*. London, Sydney and Toronto: Bodley Head.

Meek, M. (1988) *How Texts Teach What Readers Learn*. Stroud: Thimble Press.

Meek, M., Warlow, G. and Barton, G. (1977) *The Cool Web: The Pattern of Children's Reading*. London, Sydney and Toronto: Bodley Head.

Montessori, M. (1912) *The Montessori Method*. London: Heinemann.

Murray, L. and Andrews, L. (2000) *The Social Baby*. Richmond: CP Publishing.

National Institute of Child Health and Human Development (2002) *Report of the National Reading Panel, Teaching Children to Read: An Evidence-based Assessment of the Scientific Research Literature on Reading and its Implications for Reading Instruction* (NIH publication no. 00-4754). Washington, DC: US Government Printing Office.

Nawrotzki, K. (2006) 'Froebel is dead: long live Froebel!', *History of Education*, 35 (2): 209–23.

Nutbrown, C., Hannon, P. and Morgan, A. (2005) *Early Literacy Work with Families: Policy, Practice and Research*. London: SAGE.

Ockelford, A. (1996) *All Join In: A Framework for Making Music with Children and Young People Who Are Visually Impaired and Have Learning Difficulties*. Peterborough: RNIB.

Ockelford, A. (2008) *Music for Children and Young People with Complex Needs*. Oxford: Oxford University Press.

Ockelford, A. (2001) *Objects of Reference: Promoting Early Symbolic Communication* (3rd edn). London: RNIB.

Opie, I. and Opie, P. (1988) *The Singing Game*. Oxford and New York: Oxford University Press.

Ouvry, M. (2004) *Sounds Like Playing: Music in the Early Years Curriculum*. London: BAECE.

Palmer, S. and Bayley, R. (2004) *Foundations of Literacy: A Balanced Approach to Language, Listening and Literacy Skills in the Early Years*. Stafford: Network Educational Press.

Papousek, H. and Papousek, M. (1987) 'Intuitive parenting: a dialectic counterpart to the infant's integrative competence', in J. Osofsky (ed.), *Handbook of Infant Development* (2nd edn). New York: Wiley.

Pascal, C. and Bertram, T. (2006) *Connectedness, Exploration and Meaning Making, BEEL Project*. Birmingham: CREC (Centre for Research in Early Childhood).

Pearce, P. 'Writing a book', in M. Meek, A. Waiyow and G. Barton (eds) (1977) *The Cool Web: The Pattern of Children's Reading*. London, Sydney and Toronto: Bodley Head.

Piaget, J. (1962) *Play, Dreams and Imitation in Childhood*. London: Routledge and Kegan Paul.

Pinker, S. (1999) *Words and Rules*. New York: Basic Books.

Poulsson, E. (1921) *Finger Plays for Nursery and Kindergarten*. Norwood, MA: Norwood Press. (Originally printed in Boston in 1893 by Lothrop, Lee and Shepard Co.)

Qualifications and Curriculum Authority (QCA) (2005) *Continuing the Learning Journey* (from Foundation Stage into Key Stage 1). London: QCA.

Ragnarsdottir, H. (2006) 'Constructing the tools for participation in culture and democracy: children's language proficiency at age 5½ and the implications of individual variation', EECERA Conference, Reykjavik, 1 September.

Riley, J. (1999) *Teaching Reading at Key Stage 1 and Before*. Cheltenham: Stanley Thornes.

Riley, J. (2006) *Language and Literacy 3–7*. London: SAGE.

Riley, J. (2007) *Learning in the Early Years: 3–7* (2nd edn). London: SAGE.

Rose, J. (2006) *Independent Review of the Teaching of Early Reading: Final Report*. London: Department of Education and Skills.

Schneider, W., Kuespert, P., Roth, E., Vise, M. and Marx, H. (1997) 'Short- and long-term effects of training phonological awareness in kindergarten: evidence from two German studies', *Journal of Experimental Child Psychology*, 66: 311–40.

Siraj-Blatchford, I., Sylva, K., Muttock, S., Gilden, R. and Bell, D. (2002) *Researching Effective Pedagogy in the Early Years* (DfES Research Report No. 356). Norwich: HMSO.

Siraj-Blatchford, I. (2006) Conference paper presented on the findings of REPEY project at Children's Centres – improving outcomes for young children through integrated services, London, 14 December.

Siren Films Ltd. (2009) *Supporting Early Literacy: Observing Child Development*. DVD available from www.sirenfilms.co.uk

Snow, C. (2006) 'What counts as literacy in early childhood?', in *Blackwell Handbook of Early Childhood Development*, pp. 274–94. Oxford: Blackwell.

Snow, C. and Juel, C. (2007) 'Teaching children to read: what do we know about how to do it?', in M. Snowling and C. Hulme (eds), *The Science of Reading*. Oxford; Malden, MA and Carlton, Victoria: Blackwell.

Snowling, M. and Hulme, C. (2007) *The Science of Reading*. Oxford; Malden, MA and Carlton, Victoria: Blackwell.

Spencer, B., Bruce, T. and Dowling, M. (2007) 'A real achievement', *Nursery World*, 5 July: 10–11.

Spencer, L.H. and Hanley, J.R. (2003) 'Effects of orthographic transparency on reading and phenome awareness in children learning to read in Wales', *British Journal of Psychology*, 94: 1–28.

Spratt, J. (2006) 'Practical projects: birth to 5 years', in T. Bruce (ed.), *Early Childhood: A Guide for Students*. London: SAGE.

Spratt, J. (2007) Finger rhymes: why are they important?', *Early Childhood Practice: The Journal for Multi-Professional Partnerships*, 9 (1): 43–54.

Stannard, J. and Huxford, L. (2007) *The Literacy Game*. Abingdon: Routledge.

Stanovich, K. (2000) *Progress in Understanding Reading*. New York: Guilford.

Stuart, M. (2006) *Learning to Read: A Professorial Lecture*. London: Institute of Education.

Styles, M. and Bearne, E. (2003) *Art, Narrative and Childhood*. Stoke-on-Trent, UK and Sterling, USA: Trentham Books.

Tafuri, J. (2008) *Infant Musicality: New Research for Educators and Parents*. Farnham: Ashgate.

Trevarthen, C. (1999–2000) *Musicality and the Intrinsic Motive Pulse: Evidence from Human Psychobiology and Infant Communication*, Special Issue of *Music Scientiae, Rhythm, Musical Narrative and Origins of Human Communication*: 156–99.

Trevarthen, C. (2004) *Learning About Ourselves from Children: Why a Growing Human Brain Needs Interesting Companions*, Perception-in-Action Laboratories: University of Edinburgh.

Trevarthen, C. and Aitken, A. (2001) 'Infant intersubjectivity: research, theory and clinical applications', *Journal of Child Psychiatry*, 42 (1): 3–48.

United Kingdom Literacy Association (UKLA) (2005) *Submission to the Review of Best Practice in the Teaching of Early Reading*. Royston: UKLA.

Vygotsky, L. (1978) *Mind in Society: The Development of Higher Psychological Processes*. Cambridge, MA: Harvard University Press.

Walton, P., Walton, L. and Felton, K (2001) 'Teaching rime analogy or letter recoding reading strategies to pre-readers: effects on pre-reading skill and word reading', *Journal of Educational Psychology*, 93 (1): 160–80.

Whitehead, M. (2007) *Developing Language and Literacy with Young Children* (3rd edn). London: Paul Chapman Publishing.

Whitehead, M. (2009) *Supporting Language and Literacy Development in the Early Years* (2nd edn). Maidenhead: Open University/McGraw-Hill.

Whitehead, M. (2010) *Language and Literacy in the Early Years 0–7* (4th edn). London: SAGE.

Wolf, M. (2008) *Proust and the Squid: The Story and Science of the Reading Brain*. Cambridge: Lion.

Wyse, D. (2008) 'How should we teach early reading?', *Early Education: The Journal of the British Association for Early Education*, 55 (Summer): 12–13.

Wyse, D. and Goswami, U. (2008) 'Synthetic phonics and the teaching of reading', *British Educational Research Journal*, 34, 6 December: 691–710.

Wyse, D. and Styles, M. (2006) 'A response to Stuart', *The Psychology of Education Review*, 30 (2): 21–2.

Ziegler, J.C. and Goswami, U. (2006) 'Becoming literate in different languages: similar problems, different solutions', *Developmental Science*, 9 (5): 429–53.

Index

MATHEMATICS THROUGH PLAY IN THE EARLY YEARS

Second Edition

Kate Tucker *Early Years Teacher and Trainer, Exeter*

'This second edition, fully updated in line with the EYFS, has been written to help practitioners to create playful contexts to support children's independent mathematical play and learning. It provides ideas and activities but also guides the reader to sources of further information to consolidate their own subject knowledge of mathematics...The emphasis in the text and in the examples provided in this well-illustrated, informative and very practical book is on children aged from four to eight years old. This makes *Mathematics Through Play in the Early Years* particularly useful for students and teachers of children in Reception classes and at Key Stage 1' - *Early Years Update*

Teaching mathematics to young children in creative ways is made easy with this second edition of a wonderful book, which offers the reader clear advice and lots of exciting ideas to use in any early years setting.

By showing how to introduce mathematical concepts through play-based activities, this book is in tune with current thinking about best practice in teaching, and with the requirements of the Early Years Foundation Stage and current Primary National Strategy.

New material includes:

- an additional chapter on creative recording
- a whole new chapter on ways to involve parents
- discussion of policy throughout the UK
- more on using ICT
- case studies covering the whole birth to eight age range.

Essential reading for any practitioner who wants to develop their mathematics teaching, this book is equally important for all trainee teachers and early years students.

CONTENTS

Sue Rogers Foreword / Why Play? / Creating and Using a Mathematical Environment / Creative Recording and Mathematical Graphics / Counting and Using Number / Pattern / Shape and Space / Measurement / Planning, Organizing and Assessing Independent Play / Parents as Partners: Involving Parents in Mathematics and Play

March 2010 · 172 pages
Cloth (978-1-84860-883-2) / Paper (978-1-84860-884-9)

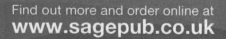

CIRCLE TIME FOR EMOTIONAL LITERACY

Sue Roffey *University of Western Sydney*

Emotional literacy has become an important issue in schools, and the ethos behind Circle Time is complementary to the thinking behind this. The Social, Emotional and Behavioural Skills curriculum (SEBS) is being established in schools, and it is recognised as contributing to a positive and successful school environment.

Offering many new ideas and activities to try out in Circle Time, this book covers:

- why your school needs Circle Time
- how you go about starting Circle Time in your school
- the underlying philosophy and basic rules
- he role of the teacher as facilitator - how you make it work
- what to do if language and attention issues are problematic
- how to tackle common problems that can occur.

The activities look at promoting listening and attention skills, self-awareness and self-esteem, class cohesion and empathy, co-operation and friendship skills.

CONTENTS
Setting the Scene / The Circle Time Framework and Getting Circle Time Going in your Class / The Basics / Circle Time Activities to Promote Communication / Self-awareness and Self-esteem / Emotional Knowledge: Understanding and Managing Feelings / Feelings of Belonging: Tuning into Others / Friendship and Cooperation / Challenges and Solutions / Useful Resources

2006 · 160 pages
Cloth (978-1-4129-1854-1) / Paper (978-1-4129-1855-8)

⑤SAGE

OUTDOOR PROVISION IN THE EARLY YEARS

Edited by **Jan White**

Outdoor education offers children special contexts for play and exploration, real experiences and contact with the natural world and the community. To help ensure young children thrive and develop in your care, this book provides essential information on how to make learning outdoors a rich and valuable part of their daily life.

Written by a team of experts in the field, this book focuses on the core values of effective outdoor provision, and is packed with ideas to try out in practice. Topics covered include:

- the role of play in learning outdoors
- meaningful experiences for children outdoors
- the role of the adult outdoors
- creating a dynamic and flexible outdoor environment
- dealing with challenge, risk and safety
- including every child in outdoor learning.

There are case studies of successful strategies in action, covering the Birth to 5 age range. Outdoor provision needs to be thoughtfully planned, well organised and appropriately supported by adults, and this book will help practitioners and students to lead good practice with confidence, so that they respond to the needs and interests of young children.

CONTENTS

Jan White Introduction / **Felicity Thomas and Stephanie Harding** The role of play: Play outdoors as the medium and mechanism for well-being, learning and development / **Liz Magraw** Following children's interests: Child-led experiences that are meaningful and worthwhile / **Tim Waller** Adults are essential: The roles of adults outdoors / **Jan White** Capturing the difference: The special nature of the outdoors / **Ros Garrick** A responsive environment: Creating a dynamic, versatile and flexible environment / **Claire Warden** Offering rich experiences: Contexts for play, exploration and talk / **Di Chilvers** As long as they need: The vital role of time / **Helen Tovey** Achieving the balance: Challenge, risk and safety / **Theresa Casey** Outdoor play for everyone: Meeting the needs of individuals / **Miranda Murray** Taking an active part: Everyday participation and effective consultation / After Word: Learning through Landscapes

March 2011 · 160 pages
Cloth (978-1-4129-2308-8) / Paper (978-1-4129-2309-5)

STUDYING CHILDHOOD AND EARLY CHILDHOOD

A Guide for Students · *Second Edition*

Kay Sambell, **Mel Gibson** *both at University of Northumbria* and **Sue Miller** *Childrens' Services, Newcastle City Council*

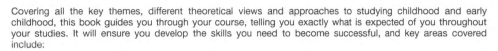

'I think this is an excellent book for childhood and early childhood students, and I can't recommend it highly enough. The authors have captured precisely the challenging issues for students, and this book really helps to develop students' understanding of the importance of knowledge and judgement in their future work with children' - *Elise Alexander, Principal Lecturer in Early Childhood Studies, Roehampton University*

Covering all the key themes, different theoretical views and approaches to studying childhood and early childhood, this book guides you through your course, telling you exactly what is expected of you throughout your studies. It will ensure you develop the skills you need to become successful, and key areas covered include:

- making the transition from personal experience of children, to studying childhood
- making the most of your lectures
- writing good assignments
- learning how to study independently
- developing your critical thinking
- drawing on the full range of student resources (people, services, research visits)
- getting a job in the early years sector.

The new edition has been thoroughly updated and now contains:

- a new chapter on placements and visits
- detailed advice on how to avoid plagiarism
- full consideration of multi-agency working, throughout every chapter
- advice on career opportunities and further study.

Designed to support students in their studies and beyond, this book is an essential purchase for anyone studying childhood or early childhood.

CONTENTS
Introduction / Key Course Themes / Reading Into Writing / Producing a Good Assignment / Visits, Observations and Placements / Doing your Dissertation or Research Project / Life Afterwards: Getting a Job and Further Study

April 2010 · 160 pages
Cloth (978-1-84920-134-6) / Paper (978-1-84920-135-3)

INCLUSIVE PLAY
Practical Strategies for Children from Birth to Eight · *Second Edition*

Theresa Casey *President of the International Play Association*

'Written from the author's deep commitment to young children's play, this second edition is straightforward and enthusiastically written and packed with good advice and activities to both enhance and challenge current play practices and adults' thinking. It's a great combination of initial theoretical justification followed by many good examples of play situations to which practitioners can relate' - *Professor Emeritus Janet Moyles, Early Years & Play Consultant*

This extremely practical and child-focused book gives you the tools you need to make sure all the children in your care are included and involved in the play opportunities of your setting.

Inside the second edition, new content includes:

- consideration of the early years curricula across the whole of the UK
- a new chapter on risk and challenge in play
- new case studies
- international perspectives
- full coverage of the Birth to Eight age range
- consideration of inclusive play from a children's rights perspective.

A key book for those in practice, and underpinned by sound theory, this book will help you encourage and support inclusive play throughout your setting; it is packed with activities for you to try, ideas for small changes to make that can have a big impact and clear guidance on writing a play policy.

With a focus on appreciating children as individuals, this book is essential for all early years practitioners and those studying early years at any level.

CONTENTS
Understanding Inclusive Play / Play Environments that Support, Intrigue, Challenge and Inspire / Enabling Inclusive Play Opportunities- The Role of Adults / Creative Input, Playful Opportunities / Risk, Challenge and Uncertainty in Inclusive Settings / Working Together / Managing for Inclusive Play

April 2010 · 136 pages
Cloth (978-1-84920-123-0) / Paper (978-1-84920-124-7)

Find out more and order online at
www.sagepub.co.uk